SHOOT TO KILL?

Shoot to Kill?

International Lawyers' Inquiry
into the Lethal Use of Firearms
by the Security Forces in Northern Ireland

Chairman:
KADER ASMAL

THE MERCIER PRESS
CORK and DUBLIN

The Mercier Press Limited
4 Bridge Street, Cork
24 Lower Abbey Street, Dublin 1

© International Lawyers' Inquiry, 1985

ISBN 978 1 78117 849 2

British Library Cataloguing in Publication Data
Shoot to Kill : report of the International
        Lawyers' Inquiry into the Lethal Use of Firearms
        by the Security Forces in Northern Ireland.
        1. Internal security — Northern Ireland.
        2. Firearms — Northern Ireland
        623.4' 4   HV8035

ISBN 978—1—78117—849—2

Contents

1. Introduction

It is easy to become cynical about the relevance of law to the conduct of security operations in what is undoubtedly an emergency in Northern Ireland. Our sensibilities are by now flooded with images of atrocities, explosions and killings committed in the name of this or that cause since the outbreak of the present stage of violence in 1969. Faced by these most gross acts of violence, it may be tempting to concede to a State the right to take whatever measures it may consider appropriate to control the situation or to extirpate the perpetrators of these crimes.

But the temptation must be sharply resisted. A State which aspires and is recognised to be part of the democratic family of nations must operate within the constraints of law, both national and international. If a State's national law and practice are inadequate in providing safeguards concerning State power, then there are international obligations which impose specific constraints on its freedom of action or establish standards which it must meet. It is no longer correct, therefore, to assert that a State is the sole judge of the efficacy or legality of measures it takes to combat paramilitary activity on its territory.

Apart from the question of legality, there is also the matter of proportionality. If the net cast to catch paramilitaries is too wide, the innocent will suffer. If the rules of evidence are changed drastically, the innocent will be convicted. If administrative measures are inadequate to investigate the lethal use of force by the security forces, the administration of justice is brought into disrepute.

This International Inquiry was therefore set up because lawyers must be prepared to assert, on behalf of people, the validity of certain basic legal rules if lawlessness is not to be permitted a blank cheque. A group of individuals cannot be expected to demand accountability from non-elected paramilitaries. But a Government in a democracy which shares certain assumptions with the four jurisdictions from which the members of this Inquiry are drawn is not only expected to abide by certain minimum desiderata but must also encourage respect for law through its policies and administrative practices.

Otherwise, there would be widespread alienation from, fear of and opposition to the machinery of law enforcement and the administration of justice.

It is this particular aspect of the situation in the North which has been confirmed by the events which have taken place since this Inquiry visited Armagh, Derry and Belfast in 1984 and took evidence from individuals – lay and expert – into allegations of the improper use of lethal force by the security forces in Northern Ireland.

The extent of public disquiet is reflected in the intervention of two senior members of the judiciary – Mr Justice MacDermott and Lord Justice Gibson – as to the way in which the British Army or the Ulster Defence Regiment or the R.U.C. may conduct themselves against either paramilitaries or alleged paramilitaries. The use of lethal force – this time causing death by plastic bullet, in the case of Seán Downes – has focused further attention on the way law is enforced in Northern Ireland and the extent of supervision and control over matters affecting life and death.

Dissatisfaction with the substantive law and its enforcement against the security forces has not been limited to political activists and concerned families only. From the testimony given to the Inquiry, it will be obvious that the anxiety is not so limited and extends further to lawyers who support the constitutional and political *status quo* in Northern Ireland. It goes even further than this, as exemplified by the resignation in August 1984 of the Coroner for Armagh, Mr Gerry Curran, after he had uncovered what he considered were 'certain grave irregularities' in the R.U.C. files concerning the death of two men.

In order to obtain the fullest possible information, the Inquiry's secretary wrote to various agencies of the British Government in the North requesting their co-operation and assistance. The collective response to this request is noted elsewhere in the Report. In any event, in advance of the response, the then Secretary of State for Northern Ireland rejected the need for any inquiry into civilian deaths at the hands of the security forces. According to the *Irish Times* (13 December 1983), Mr Prior is supposed to have said that he saw 'absolutely no necessity [for an inquiry at all]' as the previous few months have shown 'beyond peradventure that the forces of law and order are able to cope with any problems of this nature, whether it affects the Ulster Defence Regiment, the Royal Ulster Constabulary or whoever it affects.'

Such optimism concerning the machinery for dealing with 'any alleged infringements of the law by the security forces' has not been borne out by prior and subsequent events.

The Inquiry was therefore set up to investigate the extent to which the basic framework of law to govern this conduct of activities by the law enforcement agencies in Northern Ireland has been secured during the present emergency.

The members of the Inquiry, all of whom have had experience of conducting similar inquiries in other parts of the world, were deeply moved and affected by the witnesses who gave evidence and who obviously laid great store in the efficacy and value of the law as an effective instrument in regulating the conduct of the security forces. It was clear to us that the vast majority of the witnesses recognised that the State had the right to enforce the law and to maintain order. But at the same time, there was the unanimous conviction that the law must apply to all in an even-handed fashion, so as to include the dispensers of justice.

An Inquiry without a formal mandate from a Government or an international organisation is a very specific kind of legal creation. It owes its legitimacy to its performance and to the integrity of its sponsoring and disseminating process, as well as to the reputation and abilities of its members and sponsors.

It is our belief that this Report – the most comprehensive and systematic of its kind, dealing with a limited but vital aspect of the crisis in Northern Ireland – draws some important conclusions to which the two Governments with the most direct interest must give their serious attention. But in the last analysis, the Report is addressed to the peoples of these islands in whose names governments speak.

Dublin, January 1985   Kader Asmal
                                                                    Chairman

2. Background to the Inquiry

(i) The International Lawyers' Inquiry into the Lethal Use of Firearms by the Security Forces in Northern Ireland was endorsed by the following human rights organisations:

The National Council for Civil Liberties (Britain)
The Haldane Society of Socialist Lawyers (Britain)
The National Conference of Black Lawyers (U.S.A.)
The National Lawyers' Guild (U.S.A.)
The Brehon Irish Law Society (U.S.A.)
The Association for Legal Justice (Northern Ireland)

(ii) The Inquiry was initially convened by lawyers in the United States at the request of families and community leaders in Northern Ireland. Between July 1981 and February 1984 at least 20 unarmed persons were shot dead by British security forces on duty in Northern Ireland. From 1969 until 1984 reliable evidence shows that there have been over 155 'deaths in disputed circumstances', as they are classified by the British authorities. Appendix A lists the names and brief circumstances of those who have died in this way.

These deaths have led to some 14 prosecutions of members of the security forces for murder and related offences. At the time of our Inquiry no member of the security forces on duty had been convicted of murder and only one found guilty of manslaughter arising out of one of these shooting deaths.

(iii) The following law teachers and practitioners agreed to conduct the Inquiry:

— *Mr Kader Asmal (Chairman):* South African-born, and now an Irish citizen. Dean of Arts (Humanities) and Senior Lecturer in Law at Trinity College, Dublin. Mr Asmal is a barrister of Lincoln's Inn (London) and King's Inns (Dublin). He is President of the Irish

Council for Civil Liberties and has conducted human rights inquiries on Southern Africa and the Middle East.

— *Mr Geoffrey Bindman:* British solicitor (lawyer) in private practice and former legal adviser to the British Race Relations Board, the Commission for Racial Equality and the Equal Opportunities Commission. Mr Bindman has chaired Amnesty International's British Lawyers' Group and has taught in the law school of the University of California at Los Angeles.

— *Mr John Brittain:* Professor of Civil and Political Rights at the University of Connecticut School of Law and a practising attorney in the United States. Mr Brittain is Co-Chairperson of the International Section of the National Conference of Black Lawyers and active in domestic and international human rights issues.

— *M. Michel Zavrian:* Advocate in the Court of Appeals in Paris and member of the International Federation of Human Rights. M. Zavrian has played a leading role in human rights advocacy since the days of the Algerian independence struggle.

(iv) The Inquiry was assisted by two counsel from the United States:

— *Mr Richard Harvey (Secretary):* British barrister and member of the New York bar, practising law in Harlem; representing the National Lawyers' Guild.

— *Ms Marlene Archer:* National Director of the Law Students Civil Rights Research Council (U.S.A.), representing the National Conference of Black Lawyers, of which she is honorary treasurer.

Terms of Reference

(v) The Inquiry adopted the following Terms of Reference:

Having regard to international and British domestic law affecting the lethal use of firearms by the security forces in Northern Ireland, to examine:

I. The official instructions for the use of firearms by the security forces;

II. The procedures by which the security forces investigate the deaths resulting from the use of firearms by their members and the procedures they apply to deaths caused by other persons;

III. The role of the Coroners' Courts in the investigation of deaths resulting from the use of firearms by the security forces;

IV. The role of the Director of Public Prosecutions for Northern Ireland and the Attorney-General for the United Kingdom in relation to prosecutions following the use of lethal force by the security forces;

V. The effect on the civilian population generally of the use of firearms by the security forces.

Inquiry's Report: Method of Work

1. Our purpose was to gather facts; it was not our wish to be seen as a court of law. We received eyewitness accounts of a number of incidents in which civilians had been shot dead by members of the security forces and in many cases we had access to public documents, including depositions sworn to by members of the security forces.

2. During months of investigation and preparation by our legal counsel, aided by the Association for Legal Justice and many lawyers and community leaders in Northern Ireland, a representative group of cases was selected for our detailed examination. These cases were drawn from three main population centres, Armagh, Derry and Belfast, where the greatest number of deaths from the use of firearms by on-duty members of the security forces has occurred.

3. The Inquiry was sensitive to the counter-insurgency problems facing the security forces in Northern Ireland. We were therefore particularly concerned to obtain the fullest possible information from Government sources and our Chairman wrote to the following, requesting their views:

> The Secretary of State for Northern Ireland;
> The General Officer Commanding the British Army in Northern Ireland;
> The Chief Constable of the Royal Ulster Constabulary;
> The Director of Public Prosecutions for Northern Ireland;
> The Attorney-General for the United Kingdom;
> Her Majesty's Coroner for Belfast;
> Her Majesty's Coroner for Armagh;
> The Police Authority for Northern Ireland.

4. The Crown Solicitor replied as follows:

> I have been instructed to inform you that it is not the intention of any Officer of Her Majesty's Government, the Police Author-

ity for Northern Ireland, the Chief Constable of the Royal Ulster Constabulary, or the General Officer Commanding Her Majesty's Forces in Northern Ireland to submit evidence or participate in any way to the proposed inquiry referred to in your letter.

5. Our Chairman also wrote to numerous lawyers, community leaders and legal research organisations seeking their expert assistance. Their overwhelmingly helpful response and detailed written and oral submissions demonstrate the urgent need felt by many people in Northern Ireland and Britain for public accountability of the security forces where deaths result from their use of firearms.

6. A list of all individuals and organisations who provided written testimony will be found at Appendix B and a short bibliography at Appendix C. We wish to thank all who have given such invaluable help. We were impressed by the evident frankness of our witnesses, particularly those who had suffered the loss of close relatives. No eyewitness in any of the three communities which we visited had any criticism of the security forces' actions when dealing with genuine threats to life. Several witnesses paid tribute to individual police officers who had tried to help them obtain justice.

3. The History of the Use of Firearms by the Security Forces in Northern Ireland

Background to the Inquiry

7. The Inquiry was held at a time of increasing domestic and international concern at the number of civilians shot dead by members of the security forces in Northern Ireland. In 1983, Amnesty International's report for the preceding year noted:

> Towards the end of the year there were a series of incidents in which police and army personnel shot and killled unarmed suspects in Northern Ireland. Among the victims were members of the Provisional I.R.A. and the Irish National Liberation Army. There were allegations that the police had undertaken a 'shoot-to-kill' policy to eliminate supporters of these groups by killing them rather than by arrest. The killings took place in a context of repeated shootings and attacks on the police and army by supporters of these groups, and it was therefore difficult to assess these allegations.[1]

As recently as June, 1984, Mr Peter Barry, the Government of Ireland's Minister for Foreign Affairs, spoke of 'widespread concern throughout Ireland' about the circumstances of this series of killings.[2]

8. We recognise that the security forces in Northern Ireland play a counter-insurgency role which is distinct from policing functions in other parts of Ireland and the United Kingdom. The background to this role is important in understanding present-day conditions. The following summary of the historical context in which we held our Inquiry is only intended as an outline. The reader will find a bibliography of authoritative works on twentieth-century Ireland in Appendix C.

Partition and the Special Powers Act

9. The British Government partitioned Ireland in 1920. The Government of Ireland Act, passed that year by the Westminster Parliament, divided the traditional nine counties of 'Ulster', taking the six north-eastern counties and creating 'Northern Ireland'. The remaining three were integrated into the 26-county Irish Republic, or 'Irish Free State' as it was then known.

10. A civil war was fought in the Free State in which the Irish Republican Army (I.R.A.) sought to overthrow the Free State government which had signed the treaty of partition with Britain. When the I.R.A. laid down their arms the government disarmed the police force and the Irish Republic's police have remained essentially an unarmed force to this day. However, the Royal Ulster Constabulary (R.U.C.) in the North retained arms and armoured cars. The R.U.C. were assisted by a part-time special constabulary, 'the Specials', a paramilitary reserve which was eventually disbanded in 1970.

11. Northern Ireland has always been subject to emergency legislation. Among the first laws passed by the newly formed Unionist parliament was the Civil Authorities (Special Powers) Act of 1922. The Act had to be, and was, renewed annually until 1928, when it was extended for five years. In 1933 it was made permanent, remaining in force until the British Government assumed direct control of Northern Ireland in 1972.

12. Leading academic authorities on Northern Ireland's emergency powers have written:

> The powers of arrest and detention under the Special Powers Act, as it was generally known, were not formally directed against Roman Catholics and Republicans, but it was common knowledge that it was against them and them alone that it was directed and used. On each occasion that Republican militants, whether from north or south of the border, resumed their active campaign for the re-unification of Ireland by force, as in 1938 and 1956, substantial numbers of leading Republican politicians and activists were interned without trial. In this way the Unionists made use of the legal system to secure themselves both against peaceful political challenge and against internal and external terrorist attacks.[1]

13. The Act was not restricted to indefinite detention without trial; it also imposed the death penalty for some firearms and explosive offences which were not capital crimes in Britain. It permitted flogging, arrest without warrant and the prohibition of Coroner's Inquests in the interests of 'preserving peace and maintaining order' (see para. 165). In case any loophole might be found, the Unionist Government had a catch-all provision in Article 2(4):

> If any person does any act of such a nature as to be calculated to be prejudicial to the preservation of peace or maintenance of order in Northern Ireland and not specifically provided for in the regulations, he shall be deemed to be guilty of an offence against the regulations.

14. The Act remained in force throughout the Unionist Party's 60 year rule of Northern Ireland. Its operation caused Britain's National Council for Civil Liberties to compare the Unionist Party's political machine in 1936 with the fascist dictatorships then ruling in Spain, Germany and Italy.[4]

The Civil Rights Movement

15. During the 1960's, organised peaceful opposition to the Special Powers Act and to other forms of sectarian discrimination started to develop. Drawing on the example of civil rights workers in the United States, activists in Northern Ireland held marches and demonstrations to demand equal voting rights, freedom from job discrimination and equal access to government-built housing. Abolishing the Special Powers Act became a major priority since the Act was constantly invoked to ban marches, outlaw organisations and generally to give the R.U.C. and the 'Specials' a free hand in dealing with protestors.

16. In 1968 and 1969, television viewers in Britain, Ireland and further afield were shocked by newsfootage of security forces batoning peaceful demonstrators and using water cannons against them. Boyle, Hadden and Hillyard describe the events of 1969 as follows:

> The ensuing riotous confrontations in Londonderry in January and April were followed by two night-time 'invasions' of the Roman Catholic Bogside area by large numbers of uniformed R.U.C. officers in the course of which substantial damage and injury to residents was inflicted. Final confirmation for the minority community of the unity of purpose between the R.U.C., the B Specials and the Protestant militants was given by the events of August 1969 in Londonderry, Armagh, Coalisland, Dungannon, Dungiven and Belfast, which eventually led to the deployment of British troops.[5]

Evidence received by the Inquiry of Civilians killed by the Security Forces

17. .On 14 August 1969, the B Specials opened fire on a crowd dispersing peaceably following a civil rights rally in Armagh. John Gallagher was shot dead. On the same day, the British Army made its first appearance on the streets of Northern Ireland in recent years. They were sent to Derry, where the B Specials were leading a siege of the Nationalist Bogside area.

18. The Irish Information Partnership, an independent, non-profit research group based in Belgium, provided the Inquiry with extensive data on the killings of civilians by members of the security forces.[6] Their evidence shows that before the end of 1969 at least six more civilians were shot dead by members of the R.U.C. and that at least 269 persons were killed by members of the security forces on duty in Northern Ireland between August 1969 and January 1984.[7]

19. The Irish Information Partnership testified that over 155 people shot dead in this period by British soldiers and the Royal Ulster Constabulary had no manifest connection to paramilitary organisations or activities.

20. The evidence from British Government sources is contained in written answers provided by the Minister of State for Northern Ireland, Mr Nicholas Scott, who told the British Parliament on 21 March 1984:

> From 1969 to March 1984 it is believed that 233 people have been shot and killed by members of the security forces on duty in Northern Ireland.[8]

Clive Soley M.P. also asked Mr Scott how many police officers in Northern Ireland have been charged since 1969 with offences against the person, allegedly committed while on duty; how many of these were convicted; for what offences and how many were acquitted and of what charges. Mr Scott replied:

> The information requested could be obtained only at disproportionate cost.[9]

Finally, Mr Soley asked how many personal injury claims have been made for torts allegedly committed by police officers on duty in Northern Ireland and how many claims were: (a) settled out of court, and how many in favour of the plaintiff, and (b) sent to court, and how many settled in the plaintiffs' favour. Mr Scott told Parliament that:

Since April 1982, the Police Authority have received 212 civil claims for personal injuries allegedly caused by members of the R.U.C. while on duty. Since that date, 3 of these claims and 14 received earlier have been settled out of court and in the plaintiffs' favour; 1 of these claims and 9 received earlier have been settled in court and in the plaintiffs' favour.

Information on the number of claims for personal injuries received before 1 April 1982 or on the number of claims settled in court against the plaintiff since that date could be obtained only at disproportionate cost.[10]

21. The precision with which the Irish Information Partnership has recorded and presented its evidence leads us to accept their figures as more reliable than those presented by the British Government, especially in view of Mr Scott's assessment that the cost of obtaining information of great value to the public would be 'disproportionate'.

22. The Irish Information Partnership provided us with the following list:

TABLE ONE

CIVILIAN CASUALTIES CAUSED BY SECURITY FORCES
1 JULY 1969 TO 10 AUGUST 1983

	Civilian fatal casualties caused by Security Forces	Total fatal casualties caused by Security Forces	Civilian deaths by Security Forces (expressed as a percentage of total casualties caused by Security Forces
1969	9	9	100.0%
1970	5	5	100.0%
1971	33	41	80.5%
1972	39	76	51.3%
1973	15	32	46.9%
1974	7	17	41.2%
1975	3	7	42.9%
1976	9	16	56.3%
1977	3	9	33.3%
1978	4	10	40.0%
1979	0	1	0.0%
1980	6	9	66.7%
1981	12	18	66.7%
1982	5	11	45.5%
1983 (to 10.8)	4	6	66.7%
TOTAL:	154	267	57.7%

Note: The Irish Information Partnership lists as civilians only those persons 'without manifest connection with paramilitaries, security forces, police or prison services'.[11]

23. From these figures, it appears that over half of those killed by the British Army and the R.U.C. in the past 15 years have been civilians. In three years out of the last four, two-thirds of those casualties were civilians, as defined by the Irish Information Partnership.

24. Our Inquiry focuses on the lethal use of firearms by members of the security forces purporting to operate within the limits of the law. However, it is also important to record the number of, deaths caused to civilians by members of paramilitary organisations operating outside the law. Since 1969, paramilitaries have caused 1045 civilian deaths, as is shown by the following comparative table submitted by the Irish Information Partnership:[12]

TABLE TWO

CIVILIAN CASUALTIES BY VARIOUS AGENCIES FROM 1969
TO NOVEMBER 1983 (Incl.)
NORTHERN IRELAND ONLY

Killing agent	No. of civ. deaths by this agency	Total no. of deaths by this agency	Civ. as % of total deaths by this agency	Total deaths by this agency as % of total deaths in N.I.
Security Forces	155	269	57.6%	11.4%
(British Army)	(129)	(222)	(58.1%)	(9.4%)
(Ulster Def. Reg.)	(4)	(5)	(80.0%)	(0.2%)
(R.U.C. & Reserve)	(22)	(42)	(52.4%)	(1.8%)
Nationalist Paramilitary	484	1303	37.2%	57.7%
Unionist Paramilitary	561	618	90.8%	26.4%

Note: Other deaths caused by unidentified agencies are not shown.

25. The Royal Ulster Constabulary shot seven unarmed civilians in 1969. However, with the introduction of the British Army into the North of Ireland in August that year, the R.U.C.'s role in such killings was eclipsed for several years.

26. Having accounted for two civilian deaths in November of 1969, the British Army was responsible for the deaths of five unarmed civilians in 1970. All were shot in Belfast in July, during a 'curfew' imposed on the Nationalist community.

27. In 1971, however, the toll rose to 33 civilians shot dead by the British Army and, of these, 28 were shot in the period August to December. This period coincided with the re-introduction of internment without trial under the Special Powers Act. Indeed, on 9 August, when the first 342 internees were picked up,[13] eleven unarmed

civilians were shot dead before the end of that day. The Army claimed that nine, all Catholics, were shot in anti-internment riots. However, they stated that two Protestants in separate locations that day were killed accidentally. Three more accidental killings were acknowledged in the next two days, two Catholics and one Protestant. During the entire year the Irish Information Partnership records killings by the security forces under the following headings:[14]

'Riot'	13
'Accident'	13
'Gun-Battle; Crossfire'	4
(Innocent passers-by)	
'Non-Political Criminal Activity'	3
(i.e., the *Farrell* case, see below, para. 114).	

28. Within weeks of the re-introduction of internment, reliable reports were received that internees had been subject to gross physical abuse. This led the Irish Government to file a complaint with the European Commission of Human Rights at Strasbourg in December 1971, alleging torture in interrogations. Ultimately, the European Court of Human Rights ruled in 1978 that this treatment was 'inhuman and degrading' and a violation of Article 3 of the European Convention of Human Rights.

Internment was used exclusively against the Nationalist community to start with and that community responded with widespread rioting. Peaceful anti-internment demonstrations were held, but increasingly these met with bans under the Special Powers Act. Finally, on 30 January 1972, the British Army's Parachute Regiment effectively put an end to all peaceful protest by killing 13 unarmed demonstrators in Derry. A year of appalling bloodshed ensued, as can be seen from Table Three:[15]

The British Government's Reponse to Killings by the Security Forces

29. Until March 1972 the Unionist Government remained in control of security and other internal affairs. The British Army was on the streets 'in aid of the civil power' in Northern Ireland. The British Government responded initially to the developing crisis by appointing a series of special Commissions of Inquiry. Indeed between

TABLE THREE

Year	Shootings	Explosions	Persons killed		Civilians
			Br. Army	RUC/UDR	
1969	n/a	8	0	1	12
1970	213	155	0	2	23
1971	1076	1033	43	16	115
1972	10628	1495	103	43	321
1973	5018	1007	58	21	171
1974	3206	699	28	22	166
1975	1803	366	14	17	216
1976	1908	663	14	38	245
1977	1081	366	15	28	69
1978	755	455	14	17	50
1979	728	422	38	24	51
1980	642	280	16*	9*	50
1981	1142	398	23*	21*	57
1982	507	219	28*	12*	57*
1983	290*	266*	15*	18*	44*

* Note: Figures taken from Baker Report,[18] which lists Army/UDR together and RUC/RUC 'R' (Reserve) in the next column.

1969 and 1972, no less than six major judicial inquiries reported their findings. Four of these were specifically concerned with the causes of violence on the streets and with the role of the security forces. The other two investigated allegations of British Army and R.U.C. brutality in the treatment of internees detained without trial.

30. In 1969 Lord Hunt's 'Report of the Advisory Committee on Police in Northern Ireland' reported on the role of the 'B Specials' in leading attacks on Catholic/Nationalist communities:

> . . . while there is no law or official rule that precludes any person, whatever his religion, from joining the Ulster Special Constabulary, the fact remains that, for a variety of reasons, no Roman Catholic is a member.[17]

Lord Hunt found further that only 11% of the R.U.C. as a whole were Catholic. He recommended that the 'Specials' be disbanded immediately and the R.U.C. be disarmed. He proposed a re-organisation of the R.U.C. along the lines of a traditional British county police force.

31. The British government accepted Lord Hunt's first recommendation and the 'Specials' were disbanded. However, the R.U.C.

retained their firearms and no major re-organisation occurred. At the same time the Ulster Defence Regiment (U.D.R.) was created, with the same numerical strength of the 'Specials' and with many former 'Specials' enlisting.

32. The Hunt Report was followed by the Cameron Report on 'Disturbances in Northern Ireland Between October 1968 and March 1969'.[18] Lord Cameron, a senior Scottish judge, made further serious criticisms of the R.U.C. and 'Specials' for their actions in promoting civil unrest.

33. The Scarman Report on 'Violence and Civil Disturbances in Northern Ireland in 1969'[19] was not published until after the abolition of the Northern Ireland Parliament in March 1972. Lord Justice Scarman found that a number of killings by the security forces had been unjustified, including that of John Gallagher in Armagh (see para. 17 above). Despite his findings, no prosecution was brought against any member of the security forces.

34. The Widgery Report on 'the Events on Sunday 30th January 1972 which led to Loss of Life in Connection with the Procession in Londonderry on that Day'[20] has itself been the subject of further inquiries and critical reports. Lord Chief Justice Widgery criticised some of the shootings on 'Bloody Sunday' as 'reckless'. Although this would be enough to justify a charge of murder or, at the least, manslaughter, no prosecutions followed. For the most part, the Widgery Report exonerated the Parachute Regiment, although no evidence was received which supported the claim that the Army came under fire. Lord Widgery's conclusions were widely questioned in Northern Ireland and abroad.[21]

35. Following 'Bloody Sunday', widespread violence erupted and in March 1972 Westminster prorogued the Northern Ireland Parliament. The British Parliament took direct control of the entire administration of the province and promised the immediate repeal of the Special Powers Act. A new judicial inquiry was appointed under the chairmanship of Lord Diplock, one of the country's senior judges, to review the need for emergency legislation. (See para. 186 below).

36. Since 1972 there has been no government inquiry into the killing of civilians by members of the security forces. Recently, a number of leading figures in the Catholic Church and the Nationalist community have called on the Government to institute such a public inquiry, but to no avail. The refusal of the Government to appoint its

own inquiry is one of the factors which have led us to undertake our Inquiry and to present a summary of the evidence received and our findings and recommendations which follow.

Prosecutions arising from killings of unarmed civilians by Security Forces

37. The first prosecution of a member of the security forces on duty for shooting an unarmed civilian to death resulted from the killing of 12 year old Kevin Heatley on 28 February 1973. By that date, 88 civilians had already been shot dead by the Army and R.U.C.,[22] many in circumstances condemned by Coroners' Inquests or criticised in the government reports referred to in the preceding section.

38. Corporal Foxford was charged with manslaughter and convicted by Mr Justice Kelly in the Belfast City Commission (a non-jury Diplock Court – see para. 184 *et seq.*) in March 1974. The Judge found that:

> The defendant fired his rifle in circumstances where it clearly exposed others to the risk of harm and, since no reasonable person would have done so, he committed manslaughter. To fire without proper aim into a street where members of the public might have been was negligence of the grossest kind.[23]

However, three months later, the Northern Ireland Court of Criminal Appeal (Lord Chief Justice Lowry presiding) quashed the conviction on the grounds of irregular conduct by prosecuting counsel.

39. By February 1984 when we held our Inquiry, according to evidence submitted by Mr Steven C. Greer, Cobden Trust Research Student at The Queen's University of Belfast, a total of 14 prosecutions·had been brought against members of the security forces for using their firearms while on duty to kill unarmed civilians.[24] Of these prosecutions, 8 were against regular British Army soldiers, 2 against members of the Ulster Defence Regiment and 4 against R.U.C. officers. (There remains some question whether one of the U.D.R. members was on duty at the time).

40. Only one conviction was recorded prior to February 1984, that of Private Robert Reid Davidson for the manslaughter of a woman passenger in a car which passed through a checkpoint at Strabane on 12 April 1980. Private Davidson was sentenced to 12 months in a Young Offenders' Centre and his sentence was suspended for two years.

41. Of the remaining six prosecutions of regular soldiers, five resulted in acquittals and one soldier was convicted, after our Inquiry completed its hearings, of the murder of Thomas O'Reilly, shot dead on 9 August 1983. The U.D.R. officer charged with the murder of Martin Malone (see below, para. 50) was acquitted in December 1984. All four R.U.C. officers were acquitted following the Inquiry's hearings (see below, paras. 54 and 55). The trial of the U.D.R. officers for the alleged murder of Adrian Carroll, brother of Roddy Carroll (para. 54), is still pending.

Notes

1. *Amnesty International Report for 1983*, p. 290.
2. *New Statesman*, London, 15 June 1984.
3. Boyle K., Hadden T., Hillyard P., *Law and State: the Case of Northern Ireland*, Martin Robertson, London, 1975. p. 5.
4. *Report of the Independent Commission of Inquiry* established by the N.C.C.L. in 1936 to examine the administration and constitutional validity of the Special Powers Acts.
5. *Law and State*, pp. 29-30.
6. The Irish Information Partnership, located at No. 1 Morval, 7831 Gondregnies, Belgium, publishes studies of the problems of Northern Ireland and maintains a qualitative and statistical database covering political, economic, security and legal topics. It describes itself as independent of all political parties and groups.
7. *Submission of the Irish Information Partnership to the International Lawyers' Inquiry into the Lethal Use of Firearms by the Security Forces in Northern Ireland*, January 1984, Appendix VI.
8. Written Parliamentary Answer No. 124: 21 March 1984.
9. Written Parliamentary Answer No. 89: 21 March 1984.
10. Written Parliamentary Answer No. 88: 21 March 1984.
11. Irish Information Partnership, Appendix X.
12. Irish Information Partnership, Appendix VI.
13. See, e.g., Farrell M., *The Orange State*, 1980, Pluto Press. Also McGuffin J., *Internment*, 1975, Anvil Books.
14. Irish Information Partnership, Appendix VII, *Detailed Records of Civilian Casualties Caused by Members of the Security Forces in Northern Ireland*.
15. Compiled from various sources, including official government statistics cited in Boyle K., Hadden T., Hillyard P., *Ten Years On: The Legal Control of Political Violence*, 1980, London, The Cobden Trust.
16. *Review of the Operation of the Northern Ireland (Emergency Provisions) Act 1978*, (Baker Report), Cmnd.9222, April 1984, Appendix D(1).
17. Cmnd. 535, HMSO Belfast, October 1969, para. 163.
18. Cmnd. 532, HMSO Belfast, 1969.
19. Cmnd. 566, HMSO Belfast, 1972.
20. H.C. 220, HMSO London, April 1972.
21. See especially the report of Professor Dash of Philadelphia to the International League for the Rights of Man, 1972, Appendix E.
22. Irish Information Partnership, Appendix VII
23. *Submission to the International Lawyers' Inquiry into the Use of Firearms by the Security Forces in Northern Ireland*, Steven C. Greer, Cobden Trust Research

Student in Emergency Laws and Human Rights at the Faculty of Law, The Queen's University of Belfast. The facts and rationale of this case are taken from Appendix I, *A Digest of Relevant Case Law*, prepared by Mr Greer.

24. This list does not include prosecutions of members of the security forces for killings while off duty (see below, para. 46 for the conviction of a soldier for the manslaughter of Angela D'Arcy). Nor does the list include prosecutions for killings other than by firearms, as in the case of Gary English and Jim Brown, where soldiers were acquitted of a driving offence (see below, para. 179).

For the same reason, our list also omits the macabre killings of Michael Naan and Andrew Murray, stabbed to death on a farm in County Fermanagh on 23 October 1972. According to Steven Greer's written submissions, in 1978 a chance tip-off led the R.U.C. to Sergeants Byrne and Hathaway, Captain Snowball and ex-soldier Chestnutt. All were members of the Argyll and Sutherland Highlanders. Byrne and Hathaway stabbed Naan to death in an argument which arose while they were on patrol. Together with Chestnutt they killed Murray to 'shut him up' and Captain Snowball, informed of the incident, decided not to report it 'for the good name of the army and the regiment'.

Hathaway and Byrne were convicted of the murders and received life sentences in January 1981. Chestnutt was gaoled for four years and Snowball received a 12 month sentence suspended for two years.

4. Evidence

42. We held public hearings in Armagh, Derry and Belfast on 4, 5, 6 February 1984. Eyewitnesses, community leaders, church representatives and legal experts presented both oral and written evidence. We were impressed by the witnesses' frankness and sincerity and by the depth of concern felt in these cities of Northern Ireland where the greatest number of deaths in disputed circumstances has occurred in recent years.

43. Since completing our evidentiary hearings we have continued to monitor the progress of cases which we investigated and we have received reports from lawyers and researchers in Northern Ireland concerning subsequent shootings. In the following section, we set out a summary of the evidence presented by witnesses in all three communities and we have incorporated subsequent developments where known to us.

Armagh

44. The Inquiry heard evidence about the shootings of Tony Harker, Martin Malone, Liam Prince, Brigid Foster and Patrick McElhone. At the date of the hearings the cases of Seamus Grew, Roddy Carroll, Gervaise McKerr, Eugene Toman and Sean Burns were *sub judice*. However, we were able to review *in camera* the statements given to Father Raymond Murray and members of the Northern Ireland Association for Legal Justice by witnesses to those shootings. Since we completed our hearings, the officers charged with murder in those cases have been acquitted (see paras. 54 and 55) and we are therefore able to refer in our Report to this evidence and to reports of the trials.

45. We also heard from Father Raymond Murray who, since the killing of John Gallagher in Armagh in 1969, has kept detailed records of over 120 victims whom he described as:

> completely innocent people, not shot dead in cross-fire or anything like that, but (whom) I would regard as deliberately shot dead in cold blood by British Army, U.D.R. and R.U.C.

Father Murray and Father Denis Faul, who have together written many studies on the killings by the security forces, provided us with a considerable volume of written evidence in support of their oral testimony (see Appendix B). Father Murray stressed the experience of priests working in Armagh:

> Witnesses here would be very reluctant to go to the police station or co-operate with the police because of that general feeling in the community. The feeling is: 'what is the use, we will not get justice.'

He and other witnesses were particularly critical of the role of the U.D.R. since the 'Ulsterisation' policy of replacing regular British Army regiments with the Ulster Defence Regiment was introduced in many parts of Northern Ireland:

> . . . Over the years, I'm sure Father Faul and I have made a thousand complaints and nothing ever comes of these complaints. There's no outlet, there's no opening for justice and this harassment and intimidation have increased in these last few years, especially because of the withdrawal of the other British regiments from the area. . .
>   . . . We have found that, with the 'Ulsterisation', harassment has increased a lot and we just couldn't do anything about this because complaints fell on deaf ears.

Father Murray called recent visits by the British Prime Minister, Margaret Thatcher, and the Duke of Edinburgh to the U.D.R. barracks in Armagh: 'very insensitive and an insult to the Catholic community here', in view of the number of murder charges recently brought against local members of the regiment.

46. Father Denis Faul described the British Army's Special Air Service Regiment (S.A.S.) as 'basically an assassination squad' and instanced the shootings at Coalisland of Brendan McGirr and Brian Campbell on 4 December 1983. Both young men had paramilitary connections and were surprised by S.A.S. soldiers at an arms cache. They were shot dead at a time when, according to Father Faul: 'the lives of the soldiers were not at risk', confirming what he called a commonly-held view that: 'the S.A.S. don't take prisoners'.

Father Faul was also highly critical of the quality of forensic scientific evidence in many cases and urged the need for an independent forensic science laboratory. He instanced the case of Mr Michael English in Derry, who had to obtain an expert witness from Denmark in order to rebut inaccuracies in a government scientist's report on his son's death. (See below, para. 179).

Father Faul drew our attention to the killing of Angela D'Arcy in Enniskillen on 25 November 1981. Lord Justice Gibson presided over the trial of Rodney Birkitt, a British soldier who, while off-duty, had robbed and killed Ms D'Arcy in June, 1982. Judge Gibson found the soldier not guilty of murder but guilty of manslaughter. The verdict was based on the testimony of a doctor who examined Birkitt three hours after the offence and found him so drunk that, in his opinion, Birkitt would not have been capable of making a rational judgment three hours earlier. The soldier was sentenced to seven years imprisonment.

This case was not included in the statistical data of the Irish Information Partnership because the soldier was off duty. However, Fathers Faul and Murray described the impact of the case on the community as extremely serious, leaving the family: 'very displeased and dissatisfied with the conduct of the case'.

47. A former member of the British Parliament, Ms Bernadette Devlin McAliskey asserted that making formal complaints accusing the security forces of harassment or intimidation was futile. She instanced the case of Ronald Bunting, whose widow, Suzanne, gave written evidence to us about death threats made to her late husband, a Protestant Republican activist, during interrogation by R.U.C. Special Branch detectives. On his release from detention in August 1980, Mr Bunting made formal complaints to the R.U.C. and to the Association for Legal Justice. As a result, he was charged with the offence of 'wasting police time' and initially convicted. His conviction was set aside on appeal. In October 1980, Mr Bunting was murdered by gunmen in military-style uniforms who burst into his house, killing another man and severely injuring Mrs Bunting.

Ms McAliskey said that, as a former M.P., people frequently come to her with complaints against the police. She has thereby become familiar with what she describes as:

> a general sense in the Roman Catholic community that we are all guilty, only the offence has yet to be determined.

Ms McAliskey emphasised that, while it is important to consider ways of improving police complaints procedures, such changes are all very fine on paper but:

> the people with the responsibility for making those changes must have the will to make them effective.

48. We were further assisted by two practising solicitors who gave evidence in Armagh: Mr Joseph Rice of Belfast, and Mr Gus Campbell of Armagh. Both spoke of the unwarranted delays which take place in holding Coroners' Inquests when a civilian has been killed by a member of the security forces. Their criticisms and proposals are considered in detail in our chapter on Coroners' Inquests (see below, para. 161 *et seq.*).

Civilians killed by the Security Forces in and around Armagh

We set out below a summary of the evidence we received on each of the cases we examined in detail at our hearings in Armagh.

49. *Tony Harker*
Date & Place: 24 January 1982. Armagh City.
Undisputed Facts: Tony Harker, aged 21 years, was shot dead at night-time by a U.D.R. patrol in the vicinity of a supermarket in Armagh. He was unarmed and was shot in the back.
Information: Father Raymond Murray summarised the information he and the family solicitor, Mr Kieran Morgan, had discovered and members of the Harker family attended the Inquiry hearings.

There was no evidence that Harker was a member of any paramilitary organisation. He and another youth planned to break into a local supermarket at night and to steal. The side doorway was floodlit and Harker was shot as he stood illuminated there. A large quantity of blood was later found in that spot. It was alleged that no warning was given by the patrol. It was subsequently claimed he was shot while running away from the scene.

Background: Father Murray stated that Harker had complained of harassment by the R.U.C. and U.D.R. on many occasions. A few days before he was shot he reported that a U.D.R. patrol had threatened to kill him.
Official Explanation: Father Murray reported that following Harker's death the U.D.R. stated that incendiary explosions had

taken place earlier in the evening in a different part of the city. Later, they claimed that a patrol saw Harker climbing down from the supermarket roof and running into a field. Called on to stop, he continued to run. Believing that he might be an armed terrorist seeking to escape, they shot him dead in the field. Privately, however, a local R.U.C. detective told the Harker family that the shooting was in fact at the side door to the supermarket, not in the field.

Official Action: The Coroner's Inquest into the killing was adjourned a total of 8 times. The Coroner had to order the R.U.C. to re-open their investigation due to the substantial discrepancies between the security forces' evidence and the evidence provided by the family's solicitor, particularly in relation to the pool of blood by the side door. The Coroner's jury found that Tony Harker was unarmed and had been shot in the back.

Current Status: The jury recorded an 'Open Verdict' (the only verdict possible when a jury is not satisfied with the explanation given by the security forces, see para. 182). The Director of Public Prosecutions (D.P.P.) has announced that there will be no prosecutions of any member of the security forces. According to Father Murray, the general feeling in the Armagh community is that the story of Harker's running away was concocted by the U.D.R. in order to disguise the fact that they had shot a clearly unarmed man in a floodlit doorway.

50. *Martin Malone*
Date & Place: 29/30 July 1983. Armagh City.
Undisputed Facts: Malone was shot dead at night-time by a U.D.R. patrol. He was standing in front of a row of houses, together with a group of young men and women, facing towards an open field. The U.D.R. patrol demanded identification of members of the group and an argument arose. In the course of this argument one of the U.D.R. soldiers shot Malone dead. Martin Malone was unarmed.
Information: We were told by Mrs Anne McGerrigan that just after midnight she and a group of friends were sitting on a low wall near her house. A U.D.R. foot patrol came along a path by the wall and required everyone in the group to give their names and addresses. She and the others regarded this as harassment and she gave a false name while another woman refused to give any name.

At this point the husbands of two of the women in the group arrived and their wives moved to go off with them. Then one soldier pushed Bernadette Gartland with the side of his rifle against her chest. Mrs Gartland confirmed this and said her husband then told the soldier to leave her alone. The soldier replied: 'Youse are going nowhere'. Her husband and the soldier pushed each other back and forward in a short scuffle.

Mrs McGerrigan said a large number of soldiers then appeared and she was standing alongside Martin Malone. Mrs Gartland heard one of the soldiers say: 'If any one of you bastards moves, we'll shoot' and between six and ten U.D.R. members pointed their rifles straight at the group of ten or twelve young people.

Both women reported hearing the safety catches clicking off and suddenly one shot. Mrs McGerrigan was holding Malone's arm at the time and he had not stepped forward or said anything. He just fell back, dying instantly.

Brian McArdle told us how he ran to get a doctor but was stopped by a U.D.R. man who asked where he was going. 'I said: "for a doctor." He hit me with the butt of the rifle in the mouth.' All of the U.D.R. members then disappeared.

Mrs McGerrigan stayed up all night with other members of the group in her house fronting on the scene of the shooting. She told us that no police officer arrived on the scene before 6.00 am, some five or six hours later.

Father Murray sent statements from these and other eyewitnesses to the Director of Public Prosecutions on 25 August 1983, but at the time of our Inquiry, in February 1984, the D.P.P. would not confirm whether he had decided to bring charges against any person. The concern felt in the community about both the shooting and the delays in police and prosecutorial action are summarised in the following extract from the statement made by Cardinal Ó Fiaich, the Archbishop of Armagh on 1 August 1983:

> ... Martin Malone is the fourth young parishioner of mine to have been shot dead during the past year and a half by forces claiming to represent 'law and order'. After the death of Tony Harker and again after the shooting of Seamus Grew and Roddy Carroll I and several others called for a full investigation and the publication of the evidence. Now, more than six months later, we are still completely in the dark, although it was possible to investigate a similar shooting by a policeman in London in a few days.* There are some particularly suspicious circumstances in connection with the present killing: Martin Malone was shot at point-blank range. One of his comrades was assaulted
> * Reference to the Steven Waldorf shooting, see para. 123.

by a solidier as he tried telephone for a doctor; the whole patrol disappeared at once; and the police did not visit the scene of the occurrence or inform the deceased's relatives for several hours after his death.

A fortnight ago I strongly condemned the murder of four members of the U.D.R. in this diocese. How can one pronounce the deliberate killing of a member of this force as murder and the deliberate killing of an unarmed bystander as anything less than murder? It was Pope John Paul II who said on his visit to this diocese four years ago: 'I pray that nobody may ever call murder by any other name than murder'. A few weeks ago the Northern Catholic Bishops, in condemning the use of plastic bullets, had occasion to point out that there cannot be one law for the security forces and another for the public. . .'

Official Action: The Director of Public Prosecutions delayed his decision to prosecute in this case until March, 1984, more than six months after the death of Martin Malone. David Baird, a member of the Ulster Defence Regiment was then charged with the murder of Martin Malone. Instead of being remanded to the custody of the prisons department, Baird was released into military custody. Finally, in December 1984 he was acquitted of both murder and manslaughter and the Association for Legal Justice reports that he is back serving with the regiment.

Current Status: The Coroner's Inquest will be held in the near future.

51. *Liam Prince*

Date & Place: 12 June 1976. County Armagh.

Undisputed Facts: Liam Prince was shot dead at night by soldiers of the Third Parachute Regiment as he was driving his brother's car near the border between South Armagh and the Irish Republic. He was unarmed and innocent of any criminal or paramilitary involvement. He was a schoolteacher, a graduate of Queen's University and had applied to join the R.U.C., in which his father and brother were already serving.

Information: We received written and oral information concerning this killing. The Prince family home was raided by soldiers of the Third Parachute Regiment at 12.30 am on 13 June 1976. However, the soldiers' initially hostile behaviour changed as soon as they found they were dealing with R.U.C. members. They claimed that the car had been found, presumably hijacked by the I.R.A. After some time had passed, the soldiers mentioned that they had apprehended the culprit and that Liam Prince was safe. After the patrol eventually left, the family went to the R.U.C. station in Newry where they learned for the first time that Liam had been shot dead.

The soldiers who came to the house', like those security force members who went to the homes of Gervaise McKerr and Patrick Elliot (see paras. 55 and 68 below) deliberately concealed the death from the family and were apparently looking for evidence to support the theory that they had shot a terrorist.

The shooting took place at approximately 8.30 pm but the body was not removed to hospital until 2.40 am. The car stopped normally and there was no evidence of a swerve or skid as might be expected where shots are fired at a moving car. The driver's window was wound down as if he had stopped to produce his licence at a vehicle checkpoint. *Official Explanation:* The Army claimed that Prince was caught in cross-fire between soldiers and the I.R.A. They also made the suggestion that he had *failed to stop at a road-block.* However, a Captain in the Regiment subsequently stated that the trouble happened *when Liam was stopped.* Asked to clarify this discrepancy, Captain Hoyle said he was not able to discuss the 'finer details'.

The following letter was sent by the commanding officer of the Regiment to the Prince family on 18 June 1976:

> I am writing to let you know how terribly sorry I am about Liam's death at the weekend. He was a very unfortunate young man who happened to get himself in the wrong place at the wrong time and as a result became yet another unfortunate victim of this beastly campaign.
>
> I have questioned my soldiers at Forkhill very thoroughly and I do not think that in the circumstances that *(sic)* they could have done anything else. They were quite convinced that they were being shot at from Liam's car, but on closer examination it is quite clear that an I.R.A. gangster was firing at the soldiers from a little distance beyond your son's car and this is clearly why *he accelerated away from the scene.* (Emphasis added).
>
> I believe that when Captain Lewis visited you on Sunday morning he caused you some distress. I really am sorry about this. We knew at the time that your son's car had been involved in the shooting but we did not know who was in it. Our experience in the area is that young men frequently lend their cars and we were trying to establish whether your son was driving his own car or whether he had lent it. There was a fair degree of confusion at the time and Captain Lewis was only in possession of very basic information.
>
> All in all it was a very sad episode and we are all very very sorry that a good young man who was obviously not involved in the troubles in

any way should have lost his life.

Please accept my deepest sympathy in your loss

Yours ever

Peter Morton

People who live in the vicinity of the shooting have disputed this account, telling the Prince family that there was no 'cross-fire' since there was no I.R.A. activity in the area when Liam Prince was shot.

One R.U.C. sergeant told the family that his 'hands were tied' and that they would 'never get anywhere because of the controversial circumstances surrounding the shooting'.

Official Action: The family had difficulty in obtaining an inquest and the Army sought to keep the soldiers who fired from having to testify, merely submitting their affidavits. The Prince family hired a Queen's Counsel who succeeded in having the soldiers produced for questioning. An 'Open Verdict' was recorded at the Inquest. (see para. 182).

The family wrote to the D.P.P. requesting that there should be a prosecution. He never replied to their letter but it was later announced that he had decided not to prosecute.

Current Status: The authorities regard the case as closed.

52. *Brigid Foster*

Date & Place: 23 November 1983. Pomeroy, County Tyrone.

Undisputed Facts: Mrs Foster, a 78 year-old grandmother, was shot dead by an R.U.C. patrol inside a post office at Pomeroy. Members of a paramilitary organisation had staged a robbery of the post office.

Information: James Foster told us that Mrs Foster, his step-mother, had been in the post office when a group of paramilitaries arrived to rob it. From what he had been able to learn, Mr Foster said that all customers were told to crouch down and take cover. Mrs Foster's arthritis prevented her from bending. Local residents claimed that the robbers had left the post office before the arrival of the R.U.C. but that the police fired some shots into the post office, killing Mrs Foster outright.

Official Explanation: The R.U.C. put out a statement that Mrs Foster had been killed in cross-fire and they declined at first to specify who had killed her. After a delay of 48 hours they issued a further statement admitting that the fatal bullet was fired from an R.U.C. weapon.

Official Action: In August 1984 the R.U.C. informed Mrs Foster's family that there would be no prosecution.

Current Status: The inquest into Mrs Foster's death had not been held at the time of publishing our Report.

53. *Patrick McElhone*

Date & Place: 7 August 1974. County Tyrone.

Undisputed Facts: Patrick McElhone, a young farmer, was shot dead by one Private Jones on the family farm. Earlier on the same day, an army patrol had questioned him as he was driving a tractor. When he went for his tea the soldiers came to the farmhouse and ordered him outside. He was taken into a field by Private Jones. He was shot at a range of less than 20 yards with a Self-Loading Rifle (SLR). Neither Patrick nor any other member of the McElhone family had any connection with any paramilitary organisation or activity.

Information: Patrick's brother, Michael, told us that his mother saw soldiers beating Patrick after he was taken from the house and his father went out to ask them why they were doing that. One soldier then took Patrick into the middle of a meadow and ran back towards the roadway, where he turned and fired, killing Patrick. The father ran towards the soldiers, who hit him in the stomach with a rifle butt. Michael McElhone described the soldiers as not being fully in control of the situation until the ambulance arrived an hour later. He gave his evidence in a clear, restrained tone, without any apparent resentment.

Official Explanation: Private Jones made two statements, according to Michael McElhone. Initially, he claimed that the shooting had been accidental. Then he made a statement claiming that Patrick had run away from him and that he believed him to be a member of the Provisional I.R.A.

Official Action: Private Jones was charged with murder. He was tried in a Diplock Court by Mr Justice MacDermott (cf. case of *Seamus Grew,* below, para. 54.) who accepted Jones's defence that he 'honestly and reasonably believed that he was dealing with a member of the Provisional I.R.A. who was seeking to run away'. MacDermott J. accepted that, although Private Jones 'had no belief at all as to whether the deceased had been involved in acts of terrorism or was likely to be involved in any immediate act of terrorism', nevertheless the force used was no more than was reasonable in the circumstances. In defining 'the circumstances' MacDermott J. ruled that these included: 'the general wartime situation in Northern Ireland'.

Since this case was taken to the House of Lords and has had a major impact on the legality of killing unarmed civilians, we review it in further detail below in our section on international and domestic law (para. 103 *et seq.*).

Current Status: After Patrick McElhone's death, the family received an *ex gratia* (no liability admitted) payment from the British Government of £3,000. Michael McElhone told us that their mother died one month after receiving this payment and their father lived only a short while longer. His other surviving brother has been a regular patient at a psychiatric clinic since the shooting.

54. *Seamus Grew and Roddy Carroll*

Date & Place: 12 December 1982. Mullacreevie Park, Armagh City.

Undisputed Facts: Grew was driving Carroll up a hill leading to Grew's home. An unmarked police surveillance vehicle intercepted them. Police Constable John Robinson got out of his vehicle, fired his gun into the passenger side of Grew's car, killing Carroll, then went to the driver's side and shot Grew dead. Both men were unarmed.

Information: Father Raymond Murray provided the Inquiry with a number of statements given by local witnesses to the killings. He said that, following the killing of Tony Harker (above, para. 49), the local clergy and residents did not believe that the R.U.C. would investigate the killings properly. He stated that Grew and Carroll had both been subject to death threats from members of the security forces and a masked man had recently broken into Grew's home and fired shots at him while he was helping his son with his homework. Grew reported the incident but no one was arrested at the time. Instead, a week later, he himself was arrested and held for three days. On his release he filed an official complaint that R.U.C. officers had threatened him he would be 'in his box before Christmas'.

Joseph Graham, an eyewitness to the killings, gave a statement saying he recognised Grew driving up the hill at about 8.30 pm on 12 December 1982. Grew waved to him. Graham then saw another car:

> coming very fast right in behind him. There were three for definite in the car – there could have been four, but I saw just three.

He said that he believed from their clothing that the men were police but he could not see caps on their heads. As he turned to look back up the hill:

> . . . it seemed that the two tail lights behind had moved in front of him to stop him. As I said to myself: 'they have stopped Seamie', I went to walk on and I had just gone two or three steps when there was a whole burst of shooting. The shooting sounded like a big cracking noise – an awful lot of it together. Then there was a pause. The shooting stopped for a block of seconds and then there was another burst but not as prolonged as the first. The second burst sounded like two shots.

Other witnesses stated that they saw a number of people they took to be police on foot in the fields on either side of the road. In addition to the car which intercepted Grew and Carroll, another car was seen to be blocking off the bottom of the hill, preventing entrance to or egress from the housing estate.

The Very Reverend Patrick McDonnell, Administrator of St Patrick's Parish, Armagh, counted 13 bullet holes in the passenger door when he arrived on the scene. He found Carroll slumped forward in the seat and, on going to the other side of the car, he found Grew, not in the car but lying in the roadway, face upwards and apparently shot in the back of the head.

Official Explanation: The R.U.C. issued a statement claiming that Grew had driven through a police road-block, hitting and injuring a policeman, and that they had fired on the fleeing vehicle. They later admitted this was a deliberately false version of events.

Official Action (Inquest): The Coroner ruled that he could not open his Inquest until the R.U.C. completed their investigation and the D.P.P. decided whether or not to prosecute. The D.P.P., by contrast, said the question whether or not an inquest is to be held or adjourned 'is a matter for H.M. Coroner'. Nine months after the shootings neither the R.U.C. nor the D.P.P. had taken any action. They gave the Armagh Coroner no explanation for this, causing him to state in open court on 3 September 1983:

> Apart from the autopsy reports which I received from the pathologist in March, not a single statement or document has been made available to me. I have a public duty to hold every Inquest as soon as practicable and this duty has been largely negated by the unexplained delay by the D.P.P. Such unexplained delay has caused the agony of suspense and a sense of frustration to all concerned which is contrary to the principles of natural and constitutional justice.[2]

Official Action (Trial): Shortly thereafter, the D.P.P. announced that police constable John Robinson had been charged with the murder of Seamus Grew. No charge was laid in respect of Roddy Carroll. P.C. Robinson was tried in a Diplock Court at the beginning of April 1984 by Mr Justice MacDermott (see *McElhone* case above, para. 53). MacDermott J. acquitted Constable Robinson at the conclusion of all the evidence, holding that he had used reasonable force in the circumstances.

According to newspaper reports of the trial (transcripts are not made in Northern Ireland except for the purpose of an appeal), Robinson testified that he was a member of an undercover R.U.C. Special Branch surveillance team, known as 'E4A'. He and others had followed Grew and Carroll from a family funeral as they drove south into the Irish Republic to take a relative home to Monaghan. Robinson claimed an informer had told the team that Grew and Carroll planned to ferry the reputed chief-of-staff of the Irish National Liberation Army, Dominic McGlinchey, back into Northern Ireland. The London *Sunday Times* journalist, Chris Ryder, reported on 8 April 1984:

> When the Allegro (Grew's car) came back into Northern Ireland, E4A was ordered to intercept. In an unmarked car, a Special Branch inspector and P.C. John Robinson, 29, who was in uniform, cut in front of it. The Belfast Crown Court heard that P.C. Robinson got out and fired 15 times, killing Carroll. He then walked round the Allegro, unloaded [reloaded?] and fired four shots at Grew. Robinson said he believed his life had been in danger. After the shooting, a debriefing was arranged by senior officers who issued a false version of events, primarily to protect Deale, one of a group of informers on whom the Special Branch relied. . . It was not until a year later, when Robinson was forced to mount a defence to the charge of murdering Grew, that the Chief Constable allowed him to give his account of the incident.[3]

Donal O'Donnell, of the Irish *Sunday Press,* reported from the court that:

> When asked to explain forensic evidence that Grew had been shot from a distance of no more than 36 inches, and that the powder burns indicated that Grew had not been shot through the car, the Constable replied: 'My recollection is that I fired four rounds through the door'.[4]

At the conclusion of the case, according to *New Statesman* journalist, Mary Holland:

In court the trial judge praised Constable Robinson for his sharp shooting.[5]

Donal O'Donnell wrote further that:

> The verdict caused anger and dismay in the Catholic community but from past experience the British Government and the R.U.C. expected that to subside eventually, as long as the row was contained in the North.[6]

Current Status: There has been no Inquest at the time of writing. However, on 22 August 1984 it was reported that the Coroner for Armagh, Mr Gerard Curran, resigned his post due to 'grave irregularities' in the R.U.C files on the killings of Grew and Carroll.[7] The Coroner made extremely strong criticisms of the prosecuting authorities for their conduct of these cases. The following week, acting Armagh Coroner Mr James Rogers stated he would be unavailable to preside over the Grew/Carroll inquest due to 'professional commitments'.[8] The Fermanagh Coroner will now hear the Grew/Carroll inquest and the Belfast Coroner, Mr James Elliott, will preside over the McKerr/Toman/Burns inquest (see below, para. 55).

Finally, on 3 September 1984, a further postponement of the Grew/Carroll inquest was announced pending the results of an investigation by officers of the Greater Manchester police force into the R.U.C.'s investigation of the shooting and discrepancies which appeared in Constable Robinson's trial.[9]

In August 1984 we learned that a member of the U.D.R. had been charged with attempting to murder Seamus Grew at his home on 8 September 1982.

The families are understood to be considering legal action against the Government over these killings.

55. *Eugene Toman, Gervaise McKerr and Sean Burns*
Date & Place: 11 November 1982. Lurgan, County Armagh.
Undisputed Facts: Gervaise McKerr was driving his car with Toman as the front seat passenger and Burns in the back. An R.U.C. patrol opened fire on the car, killing all of the occupants. Eugene Toman was half out of the passenger door when he was killed. All three men were unarmed.
Information: The Association for Legal Justice provided us with the statements which they had obtained from witnesses within a few days of the shootings. One witness, who requested that his name be withheld, recalled seeing two police cars in a lay-by on the Tullygally

East Road as he drove past at about 7.30 pm. On his return journey, at about 9.05 pm, he noticed that only one police car was in the lay-by and that there was no road-block. Not long after passing the spot he heard shots:

> At first I thought it was someone hammering on tin but as it continued I ran to the door. The shooting was still going on. It sounded like rapid fire, it stopped for seconds, then there were a series of single shots, between 10 and 15, then a pause, then a series of single shots again.

The car came to a stop some 300 yards from the junction of the Tullygally East Road and the Portadown Road. This was significant to witnesses at the scene who say that there was no road-block mounted by the R.U.C. They emphasise that some 40 bullet holes were found in and around the driver's door and McKerr, the driver, had suffered devastating injuries. It would have been quite impossible for him to have continued to drive between 250 and 300 yards on a winding road – the distance between the alleged road-block and the point where his car came to rest.

After the shooting, the R.U.C. raided the home of Mr McKerr's wife, Eleanor. In the course of a thorough search, they asked her if she knew where her husband was, which she did not. According to the witnesses, at no time did they inform her that he had been shot dead.

Official Explanation: The R.U.C. issued a statement claiming that the car accelerated through a checkpoint at the junction of the Tullygally East Road and the old Portadown Road. They said that police at the checkpoint opened fire, the car careered off the road and when they went to examine it the occupants were all dead. At a later stage, police claimed that they believed that gunfire was being returned but subsequent examination had revealed that this was the effect of low velocity rounds striking the car's rear window and giving off flashes.

Official Action: Following the statement of the Armagh Coroner, (See above, para. 54) the D.P.P. announced, almost a year after the killings, that three R.U.C. officers had been charged with the murder of Eugene Toman. There was no charge in relation to either McKerr or Burns, because the prosecution claimed that, since Toman was found half out of the car, he must still have been alive when the car stopped and he was killed as he tried to crawl out of it.

Official Action (Trial): We have again been forced to rely on newspaper reports of the trial because transcripts are unobtainable.

The trial of Sergeant William Montgomery, Constable David Brannigan and Constable Frederick Robinson took place in a Diplock Court before Lord Justice Gibson in June 1984. At the close of the prosecution case the judge announced that he intended to acquit all three men. He then adjourned the case until the following day when he gave detailed reasons for his decision:

> I wish to make it clear [Judge Gibson said] that having heard the Crown case I regard each of the accused as absolutely blameless in this matter. That finding should be put in their record along with my own commendation for their *courage and determination in bringing the three deceased men to justice, in this case, the final court of justice.*
>
> Those who brought the prosecution on such evidence [the judge continued] undoubtedly did not take into account that these men's personal security was at risk. . .
>
> The case is going to have a more widespread effect among other members of the security forces generally. When a policeman or soldier is ordered to arrest a dangerous criminal and on the basis of that order to *bring him back dead or alive*, how is he to consider his conduct now?[10] (Emphasis added).

Evidence: In the course of the trial Mr Michael McAtamney a senior Deputy Chief Constable in the R.U.C. gave evidence that the three accused, like P.C. Robinson in the Grew case, were all members of the undercover 'E4A' surveillance unit, trained by the S.A.S. in 'firepower, speed and aggression'. The *Irish News* reported that Mr McAtamney told Judge Gibson that the officers' training was based on the premise:

> Once you have decided to fire, you shoot to take out your enemy.
> 'Do you mean, permanently out of action?' asked the judge.
> 'Yes,' replied Mr McAtamney.[11]

According to the evidence, the E4A unit had been tailing the three deceased men for three days. However, since the judge acquitted at the close of the prosecution case, the three accused did not give evidence. There is thus no finding by the court, unlike Robinson's case, about the truth of the claim that the deceased had driven through a vehicle checkpoint.

The reason given for the cover-up story in the killings of Seamus Grew and Roddy Carroll was the need to protect a Special Branch informer. A similar cover-up was admitted in the present case and the *Irish News* reported that:

It was also learned that the three [officers] did not tell detectives who questioned them about the shooting about this undercover operation, and had claimed they were on a normal R.U.C. patrol.

Sgt Montgomery only told the interviewing officers about this after a letter was read to him and the constables by R.U.C. Deputy Chief Constable Michael McAtamney that they were no longer bound by the Official Secrets Act.[12]

The defence was similar to that of P.C. Robinson in that the officers alleged that they had information that Toman and Burns were probably armed and on their way to commit a murder.

Although evidence was given that two of the three men were wanted for multiple murder, no explanation was given why the R.U.C. continued to tail the men for three days instead of arresting them.

Following the acquittals, Lord Justice Gibson's remarks were condemned by the Irish Government, elected representatives of the Nationalist community in the North and lawyers in Northern Ireland and Britain. However, he also received praise from Unionist politicians. He then took the unprecedented step of summoning a press conference in his chambers at which he denied the allegation that he supported a 'shoot-to-kill' policy:

> I do not believe that on any fair analysis my words were capable of that interpretation [he said]. Indeed, nothing was further from my mind, nor would I or any other judge contemplate for a second that such a view was tenable.[13]

Current Status: An Inquest was scheduled for September 1984. However, the Armagh Coroner, Mr Gerard Curran announced his resignation on 22 August, having reviewed the R.U.C. files in the Grew and Carroll killings (para. 54) and finding such 'grave irregularities' that he was not prepared to preside at the inquests in these cases.[14] On 29 August it was announced that the acting Armagh Coroner who replaced Mr Curran would be unable to preside over the inquests due to 'professional commitments' and that the Belfast Coroner, James Elliott would preside over the inquest into the deaths of Eugene Toman, Sean Burns and Gervaise McKerr.[15] No reason was given why this inquest would not be held by the Coroner who will preside over the Grew and Carroll inquest.

The calls for Lord Justice Gibson's resignation and the controversy about the case continue. In its leading editorial on 11 June 1984, the *Irish Times* wrote:

Mr Peter Barry [The Irish Foreign Minister] was right to protest to the British Ambassador about the extraordinary remarks of Lord Justice Gibson when he acquitted the R.U.C. men accused in the Armagh 'shoot-to-kill' case. He had a right, too, to demand action to make it clear that a 'shoot-to-kill' policy is not being pursued; and he certainly had every right to vindicate the prerogative of the Irish Government to speak up for the harassed nationalist community in Northern Ireland.

Dublin's 'legitimate interest' in Northern affairs has been accepted by several British Governments, including the present. Dublin is a partner – one of the chief partners – in the search for a political settlement. And Dublin has an intense interest in the kind of security policies (to dignify them by that word) pursued in the North.

The editorial concluded by calling on Mr James Prior, Secretary of State for Northern Ireland, to prove his concern by:

> . . . reforming the system of justice in Northern Ireland, abandoning the 'shoot-to-kill' tactic and disbanding what in Latin America would be called 'death squads'.[16]

Derry

56. In Derry we heard evidence relating to the killings of Eamonn 'Bronco' Bradley, Neil McMonagle, Denis Heaney and Patrick Duffy. We also heard testimony regarding the Coroner's Inquest in the case of *Gary English,* (see below, para. 179).

57. We were well aware of the especial concern of the people of Derry since the events of 'Bloody Sunday' in January 1972 when, in the words of the submission of Boyle, Hadden, Greer and Walsh to the Baker Committee:

> The [13] deceased were killed when paratroopers opened fire on a largely peaceful anti-internment rally in Derry. The military witnesses (to the Widgery Tribunal – see above, para. 34) alleged that every one of the dead and wounded was a gunman or nail or petrol bomber. All the civilian witnesses testified that none of the dead or injured was in possession of a gun or bomb. The civilian witnesses included many British, Irish and foreign journalists.[17]

Although the Widgery Tribunal[18] concluded that the army was fired on first, it was unable to say with certainty whether any one of the deceased or wounded had been shot whilst holding a gun or nail bomb. Shooting in one locality was described as 'reckless' by Lord

Widgery; however, no prosecutions followed. Professor Samuel Dash's Inquiry for the International League for the Rights of Man found that the evidence pointed to the army firing first and that the Widgery Report contained significant procedural and substantive flaws.[19]

58. Mrs Kathleen Gallagher, a resident of Derry, told us of the continuing high level of concern in the region, saying that:

> . . . since 1970 there has been a litany of deaths within the Derry area, of assassinations by the British Army in different guises – U.D.R., R.U.C., S.A.S.

Mrs Gallagher referred to the killing of Kathleen Thompson, a housewife killed in Derry by the British Army. She said Mrs Thompson was found still clutching the lid of her dustbin, which she had reached for, in order to alert the neighbours to the presence of the Army and the probability that house raids were about to occur. That death, in November 1971, was listed by the Army as an accident but was not viewed as such by Mrs Thompson's community.

According to Mrs Gallagher, the failure to prosecute in such cases has left many people in Derry with the impression that the security forces are not amenable to the ordinary law.

59. *Neil McMonagle*
Date & Place: 2 February 1983. Shantallow, Derry City.
Undisputed Facts: McMonagle was shot dead by a plain clothes soldier who also seriously wounded McMonagle's colleague, Liam Duffy. Duffy and McMonagle had approached a man at the rear of a house in which they were babysitting at about 9.30 pm. Having shot them, the man left the scene as civilians came to investigate what was happening. Uniformed soldiers quickly arrived. They prevented an ambulance from reaching the two men until the R.U.C. arrived. When Father Carolan, a local priest, asked the soldiers to let the ambulance through they refused. McMonagle died at the scene but Duffy survived. No weapons were found near either body.
Information: We were provided with a copy of the book of evidence (sworn witness statements) prepared by the R.U.C. for the trial of

Liam Duffy, who was charged with possession of firearms and explosives found buried a short distance from the scene of the killing. No weapon was found at the point where the men were shot.

Two of McMonagle's brothers described how R.U.C. detectives had threatened each of them on separate occasions. They said they were told that the officers intended to kill Neil McMonagle if they ever got their hands on him. Jim McMonagle said they told him:

> If we see him with you and your wife and your children in the car, the whole lot will get it.

A number of witnesses said McMonagle was being followed by the security forces and that he knew this.

From the book of evidence it appears that, before the night of the shooting, McMonagle and Duffy had buried some ammunition and weapons in nearby fields. On 2 February 1983, as they were babysitting for a friend, they went to investigate on seeing a man prowling outside. McMonagle approached a man standing near a fence facing across an area of open ground.

'Soldier A', as that man is described in the book of evidence, has never given testimony about what happened. In his statement, writing of McMonagle, 'Soldier A' claimed:

> . . . The same male who had spoken and was familiar to me, came towards me and as I passed him he came behind me and I could see him drawing what I could clearly see was a pistol from the waistband of his trousers with his right hand. This came from the front/right of his waistband and from under his coat. At the same time he reached out with his left hand and caught me from behind on the left shoulder. I could feel he had put the pistol into the small of my back.

He claimed the two men then made him walk towards a fence:

> It was about this time that I realised that as soon as I got to the fence I was a dead man. I knew they would have found my gun, personal radio and identification card easily and I would have been shot. The way the male was advancing towards me from my left front (Duffy) . . . I was sure he was armed with a gun. I knew I had to act before I got to the fence so I drew my Browning pistol with my right hand from the front waistband of my trousers and immediately fired two rounds at the advancing male in front of me. This was a single-handed grip, because at the same time I knocked the gunman's right hand away from my back using my left arm and then immediately swivelled around and fired two rounds with my outstretched right hand into the gunman who was behind me. Both of these males fell to the ground.

When Duffy pleaded with him not to shoot him again and told him his own and McMonagle's names, 'Soldier A' then said that he 'immediately realised that this person was a known terrorist who was "on the run" and a member of the I.N.L.A. This was probably why his face was familiar to me.'

Members of McMonagle's family testified that they believed the soldier's presence near the house was no accident and that a deliberate trap had been laid to lure McMonagle to his death and leave no independent witnesses. Liam Duffy's mother also testified that people in the locality believed that it was only the sudden arrival of neighbours who had heard the shots which saved Liam Duffy's life.

Official Explanation: The R.U.C. stated that McMonagle was a known member of the I.N.L.A., wanted for murder. They claimed he was killed by the soldier in self-defence.

Official Action: The Inquest was held, after the conclusion of our hearings, on 26 April 1984. Soldier 'A' did not attend to answer questions but instead his statement was read out. A detective inspector in the R.U.C. testified that there was no evidence other than Soldier 'A's' word that McMonagle was armed.[20]

The family's lawyer, William Hasson, suggested to the coroner that, if Soldier 'A's' story that he shot McMonagle at point-blank range were true, then traces of residue from the discharge of his gun would have been found on McMonagle's clothing. The pathologist found no such traces.

The jury found that McMonagle died as a result of a bullet wound to the chest. The coroner, expressing sympathy with the deceased's family, said that while people believed that such incidents would be forgotten in the passage of time, relatives would have to live with this for the rest of their lives.[21]

In December 1983 Duffy pleaded guilty to possession of explosives and weapons found near the scene but unconnected with the killing. He received a seven year prison sentence. Duffy was never charged with any offence connected with Soldier 'A's' evidence, such as attempted murder, assault with a deadly weapon or possession of a weapon with intent. His family and even their solicitor were excluded from the Diplock court room, allegedly because of lack of space.

The D.P.P. has ruled that there is to be no prosecution of any member of the security forces for the killing.

60. *Eamonn 'Bronco' Bradley*

Date & Place: 25 August 1982. Rear courtyard of Shantallow House public house in Derry City.

Undisputed Facts: Bradley was shot dead by Privates Jones and Bailey of the Second Royal Anglian regiment at approximately 5.00 pm shortly after leaving the public house. He was killed by two high velocity bullets from behind which entered his brain and heart. They were fired from a distance of some 130 feet. Bradley, who was aged 23, had left the public house with a friend, Paul McCool. There was no alcohol in his body and he was unarmed.

Information: We received a copy of the book of evidence prepared for the trial of the two soldiers who were charged with his murder. Paul McCool and Michael Bradley, the deceased's brother, claimed that a number of death threats had been made to the deceased by members of the security forces before the shooting. We visited the site where the shooting took place.

McCool and other friends of Bradley had been arrested about two weeks previously. They were interrogated by the R.U.C. and released without charge. McCool told us that detectives had said:

> If we can't get you in the courts, we'll get you on the streets.

McCool and Bradley, like the majority of young Catholic males in Derry, were unemployed. They normally spent afternoons in the bar talking and playing a poker machine. Every day, Bradley would leave at 5.00 pm to go home for tea. The day before the shooting, Bradley and McCool were stopped at that time by the R.U.C. as they left the bar. After an identification check they were allowed to go.

On 25 August, a major search of the building next door to the bar was conducted by the army. Bradley was walking slightly in front of McCool as the two of them left the bar at 5.00 pm. They started to walk across the rear courtyard when McCool was intercepted by a soldier and his view of what happened next was obstructed. No one attempted to stop Bradley, who continued walking. The soldiers' written statements all contradicted each other. However, one local resident described in her statement seeing Bradley through her window. He had his hands in his pockets and:

> when they were roughly level with the back of my neighbour's car he took his hands out of his pockets and started to run to my left, that is towards the gable end of the houses, he then went out of my sight. I heard one soldier, this was the one in the middle of the car park, shout to halt. . .

> At this stage things got a bit confused, but I thought something was about to happen, I tried to get my two children into the kitchen. I heard somebody shout: 'stop you bastard' and the sound of three shots. I can't say in what order these things happened. . . I would like to say that at no time did I see Bronco with a gun. One last thing, the shots I heard, I think I heard one shot then a slight pause and two or more close together.

Paul McCool told us he was certain that no warning was given until after the first shot had been fired.

Official Explanation: The R.U.C. issued four bulletins on the shooting.

In the first statement, issued shortly after the shooting at 5.15 pm it was claimed that members of a British Army patrol had been fired on in Shantallow; that the patrol had returned fire and that they had claimed one hit.

The second statement, issued a short time later, said members of a British Army patrol had been involved in a shooting incident in which one man had been fatally injured. Then, a third R.U.C. statement said that the police were investigating circumstances surrounding the shooting and that there had been no reports of any shots being fired at the patrol.

Finally, about midnight, the police explained that the patrol had been about to start a search operation at Racecourse Road when the shooting occurred. 'No firearms were found at the scene and the deceased is believed to have sustained two bullet wounds,' the statement added.[22]

The R.U.C. also claimed that Bradley was 'wanted' on serious terrorist charges. They did not explain why he had not been arrested the previous evening when stopped and checked by the R.U.C.

Official Action: Privates Jones and Bailey were questioned by the R.U.C. within a few hours of the shooting. Both soldiers asked for and obtained legal advice within three hours and all questioning was suspended until the Military Legal Adviser arrived.

The soldiers were not formally arrested and charged until 4 October 1982. Their trial was conducted in a Diplock Court in September 1983 by Lord Justice Gibson (see para. 55 above). Neither Jones nor Bailey ever reached the point of testifying, as the judge held at the conclusion of the prosecution evidence that there was insufficient evidence that the force used was more than that which was reasonable in the circumstances. The Judge therefore acquitted both soldiers.

In his interview with the police, Private Jones had said he saw two men walking from the pub and he heard his commander say to them:

> . . .something like, 'Wait a minute'. Two men broke out into a quick trot. L/Cpl Barloga shouted to the men: 'Halt or we'll fire.' We usually say this as a warning command to them. I think I heard a second boy say this but I don't know which one. One of the boys broke out into a much faster run and said something like, 'I've got to go home.' I've no idea what the other boy did. My eyes were firmly fixed on this one boy. The boy sort of pointed with his left hand towards the alley way.
>
> I could see the boy – he was turned that I could see the front part of his body from right shoulder across to his left. His body was sort of half turned. He brought his left hand down to the waistband area of his body. The movement seemed purposely made. At the same time his body turned slightly away from me to his left. I though he was getting a pistol or gun from his trouser waist band. I assumed he had a holster on his trousers.
>
> A second warning was shouted a few seconds after the first warning was given. This was a fraction of a second before he brought his hand down. The second warning was something like, 'Stop you bastard'. I can't say for sure who said that. Then I heard a weapon being cocked as the warning, 'Stop you bastard', was given. I then cocked my weapon and I remember hearing another weapon being cocked about the same time. As his hand came down I brought my weapon to the aim.
>
> I aimed at his knees because my weapon isn't zeroed all right. In Northern Ireland training we're told to shoot two well aimed shots and find the best cover position just in case. I fired two well aimed shots at the boy's knees. I didn't hear any other shots besides my own. I saw the boy jump up, his right knee sort of came up harder as though he had been shot in the leg. He sort of buckled over and fell to his side and lay there.

Private Bailey stated that they started to pursue Bradley and cocked their rifles. Then:

> . . . I saw the youth reach across his body with his left hand and at the same time I saw him glance to his right just then I heard two rifle shots to my right which I knew to be army shots. I then immediately fired one shot from my SLR Rifle at the youth's waist and I saw him fall near the entrance of the alley way. I then went and got the other youth by the blue car and searched him.

There are many discrepancies between the versions of events given by each member of L/Cpl Barloga's unit. We recognise that the circumstances of a shooting make it difficult to remember precise sequences of events. However, the inescapable facts are that, having shouted: 'Stop you bastard,' the soldiers, one armed with an inaccurately sighted SLR, shot and killed an unarmed man who was running away from them. Although the soldiers claim to have fired aimed shots at Bradley's waist and legs, he was hit in the brain and heart.

Current Status: At the time of our hearings, no Inquest had been held into the killing. The family informed us that they are awaiting the outcome of the Inquest before bringing a civil action against the British Government.

61. *Denis Heaney*

Date & Place: 10 June 1978. Chamberlain Street, Derry City.

Undisputed Facts: Heaney was shot dead by undercover plain clothes soldiers from an unmarked military patrol car in the early afternoon in Derry's city centre.

Information: Denis Heaney's two surviving brothers attended the Inquiry at very short notice. They stated that Denis Heaney had been arrested two to three weeks before his death and held in Strand Road Police Barracks for three days' interrogation. They said the R.U.C. told him they would pick their time and then shoot him because they believed him to be an I.R.A. volunteer.

After the interrogation Heaney was examined by a doctor, whose report supported Heaney's claim that he had been lifted by his mastoid bones (behind the ear), spun around and punched in the stomach and the side of the head.

We were told that two cars pulled up alongside Heaney as he was walking in the city centre and that civilian witnesses saw him walk across the road. Plain clothes soldiers got out of their unmarked car and shot him dead. The driver of a second car then opened his door and fired more bullets at him.

Official Explanation: The army claimed Heaney was shot while trying to hijack an unmarked military patrol car.

Official Action: There was no prosecution. The Inquest occurred 18 months after the shooting. The family retained a Queen's Counsel who persuaded the Coroner to refuse to accept written statements from the undercover soldiers. The army claimed in a statement that they had retrieved a gun from Heaney's body. However, no gun was produced at the Inquest. Although civilian eyewitnesses had given full statements to the police, the brothers told us that these witnesses were not called at the Inquest. The Coroner's jury recorded an 'Open Verdict'. (See para. 182).

Current Status: The family is taking legal action against the British Government and claims that they are facing deliberate harassment from the R.U.C. We were told that the police chose the anniversary of Denis Heaney's death to return his clothes to the family.

62. *Patrick Duffy*
Date & Place: 24 November 1978. In a deserted house in Derry City.
Undisputed Facts: Mr Duffy's widow, Moira, testified that he was an 'auxiliary member of the Provisional I.R.A.', who had gone to an arms dump in a disused house to retrieve some guns stored in a wardrobe. An undercover army patrol keeping watch on the house shot Duffy dead inside the house.
Information: When Patrick Duffy arrived to pick up the weapons, he entered the darkened room and approached the wardrobe. According to Mrs Duffy, the wardrobe door was still shut and Mr Duffy did not have any weapon in his hands when undercover soldiers concealed in the darkness opened fire on him, leaving 14 bullets in his body, with 38 more having passed through him.
Official Explanation: The army claimed Duffy was shot after picking up a gun at the arms dump. No explanation was given why the soldiers waited until Duffy had a weapon in his hands instead of arresting him as he entered the house.
Official Action: There were no prosecutions. At the Inquest the statements of 'Soldiers A, B, and C' were read out and Mrs Duffy's barrister had no opportunity to cross-examine them on their reasons for killing her husband.
Current Status: We were told that no prosecutions were ordered and that no civil action had been taken. The matter is evidently regarded as closed.

Belfast

63. In Belfast we held two sets of hearings. First we met lawyers and representatives of various organisations including: the Association for Legal Justice, represented by Seán McCann and Ann Murray; the Committee for the Administration of Justice, represented by Dr Tom Hadden of the Faculty of Law, Queen's University, Belfast; the Northern Ireland Association of Socialist Lawyers, represented by Norman Shannon and Seamus Treacey; the Northern Ireland Civil

Rights Association, represented by John Watson; Steven Greer, Cobden Trust Research Student at Queen's University, Belfast and Pascal O'Hare, Jonathan Taylor and Joseph Rice, all solicitors in private practice in the city.

64. The object of this first session was to obtain as much detailed evidence as possible on the extent to which legal restraints exist in practice to control the use of firearms by the security forces.

65. The second session of the Inquiry in Belfast heard oral evidence about the killings of Danny Barrett, Patrick Elliot, Maura Meehan and·Dorothy McGuire. Written submissions were received on the deaths of William Millar, Tony Dawson and Francis McColgan in all of which prosecutions were pending. Further written materials were provided by the Association for Legal Justice concerning the 1972 shootings in Belfast of the college students Patrick Magee, who was killed, and Francis McGuinness, injured in the same incident.

Legal Restraints and Remedies

66. The lawyers and community representatives who attended the first Belfast session were unanimous in criticising the inadequacies of the Coroners' Courts. They believe that undue delay, inadequate investigation, exclusion of material evidence and restrictions on the powers of the jury are preventing Coroners' Inquests from fulfilling their statutory functions.

In our chapter on Coroners' Inquests, below at para. 161, we refer extensively to the detailed submissions prepared by these witnesses.

They expressed equally strong criticisms about the refusal of the House of Lords and other courts to provide a clear interpretation of Section 3(1) of the Criminal Law Act (Northern Ireland) 1967. This section permits the security forces to use 'such force as is reasonable in the circumstances' to prevent crime or make a lawful arrest.

In paras. 103 to 145 below we consider in detail the extremely broad scope given by the Northern Ireland judiciary to 'reasonable force' and 'the circumstances'. The Northern Ireland Association of Socialist Lawyers stressed that control of the use of firearms by the security forces is ultimately a political, rather than a legal problem. They argued that there is:

> no desire by the authorities actually to deal with abuse by the security forces.

Several of our witnesses observed that the absence of democratic accountability of the security forces has led to a weakening of public confidence. For example, when R.U.C. officers investigate a shooting by another member of the R.U.C. this cannot be viewed as impartial or fair, especially when the member in question is almost invariably exonerated.

Witnesses questioned the capacity of the R.U.C. to investigate shootings by the British Army and Ulster Defence Regiment and our attention was drawn to a recent case which highlighted this problem: Mr Justice Hutton in *Lynch* v. *Ministry of Defence,* (1983) 6 N.I.J.B., criticised an entry in the battalion log of the King's Own Scottish Border regiment. The judge said (at p. 16):

> The entries for the entire night of 22nd September 1976 contain references to the shooting at the car in Norglen Parade and to Alexander Lynch being admitted to hospital. Then at 23.54 hours there is the entry of the following message from Brigade to the headquarters of the Company to which the soldiers belonged:
>
> > Soldiers involved in incident not to be interviewed by R.U.C. – R.U.C. want to interview them, stall them – telephone me and I will dispatch Flying Lawyer.
>
> The Court deprecates this message. It is the function of the police to investigate shootings, including shootings where it may ultimately become apparent that soldiers opened fire lawfully, and the military authorities should assist the police to carry out such investigations.

Alexander Lynch claimed damages from the Ministry of Defence as a result of being shot by soldiers as he drove through a Belfast checkpoint on 22 September 1976. Mr Justice Hutton, having refused to award damages to Mr Lynch, reportedly added:

> The effectiveness of checkpoints against the terrorist campaign in Northern Ireland would be very greatly reduced if the law did not permit the security forces to fire at a driver who deliberately ignored a clear signal to halt and whom the security forces reasonably believed to be a terrorist. 'Terrorists could then drive through blocks with a considerable degree of impunity'.[23]

The Inquiry was also referred to an earlier judgment of Lord Chief Justice Lowry in *R.* v. *Foxford* [1974] N.I. 181 at 200:

> ... from September 1970 until September 1973 an R.U.C. Force Order
> was in operation whereby if an offence against the ordinary criminal
> law was alleged against military personnel in Northern Ireland the
> interviewing of military witnesses and of the alleged offender himself
> was conducted exclusively by military investigation. This practice has
> been discontinued, but we deprecate this curtailment of the functions
> of the police and hope that the practice will not be revived.[24]

However, we were told by more than one lawyer that this practice
has not disappeared. The only satisfactory solution, it was urged on
us, would be an independent investigative body, comparable with
the Procurator Fiscal in Scotland or the Special Prosecutor in the
United States. Nothing less would ensure the zeal and impartiality
which are vital.

More detailed representations made during this informative session of the Inquiry are incorporated into our Report under each
chapter heading and the extensive written materials provided by our
witnesses are listed in Appendix B.

We now turn to the oral evidence heard in our second session of
Belfast hearings.

Belfast Case Summaries

67. Danny Barrett

Date & Place: 9 July 1981. Ardoyne, Belfast.

Undisputed Facts: Danny Barrett, aged 15, was shot dead by a British
Army sniper at about 9.30 pm as he sat on his front garden wall.
He was unarmed. Neither Danny Barrett nor any member of his
family had ever been involved in any paramilitary organisation. On
the preceding day an I.R.A. prisoner, Joe McDonnell, had died
on hunger strike and rioting occurred in the Ardoyne and other areas
of Belfast. Danny took no part but sat on the wall with a friend,
talking to his father who stood in the doorway to their home.

Approximately 75 yards east of the Barrett home some shots were
fired at an R.U.C. landrover. A soldier stationed at an army observation post in the Flax Street Mill, some 260 yards south of where
Danny Barrett was sitting, looked through the magnifying sights on
his rifle and shot and killed Danny Barrett.

Information: We were supplied with the findings of the Coroner's
jury and statements and other documents available at the inquest.
Father Faul and Father Murray, in their booklet: *Danny Barrett: A
British Army Murder*, described an Army search of the Barrett home

immediately after the shooting, writing that an officer in charge of the search had to order his men to stop looking through children's schoolbooks and to search for a gun. No gun was found.

Danny died almost instantly, so no surgery could have saved him. However, we were told that, on the way to the Mater Hospital, the ambulance carrying him was stopped by the British Army and the occupants were questioned for about three minutes. The ambulance then continued for a further 50 yards or so before being stopped again by the Army. Despite the ambulance crew's protests, a further three minutes were spent in questioning. 150 yards further on, the ambulance was stopped by the R.U.C. who, after a further series of questions, finally escorted them to the hospital.

The Inquiry heard from volunteer ambulance driver Gerard McGivern that the practice of stopping ambulances on emergency missions is 'quite usual' in some areas and he described it as 'absolutely unacceptable'.

Official Action: The Director of Public Prosecutions announced that 'Soldier A' would not be prosecuted. No reason was given for the decision and we were unable to discover any official explanation by the Army or the D.P.P. for the soldier's action.

Inquest Reports: We received copies of the sworn depositions prepared for the Coroner's Inquest, as well as newspaper reports of the proceedings.

The Inquest was not held until August 1982, over 13 months after the killing. The Belfast Coroner, James Elliott, refused to compel the attendance of 'Soldier A' who had fired the fatal shot. He allowed his written statement to be read. In that statement the soldier claimed:

> I saw what I believed to be a person standing in the gardens of Havana Court. He was holding a rifle in the firing position at the hip. He appeared to me to have just fired the shots as the smoke was still milling around him. I fired one round at this person and I saw him fall back in the gardens. . .
>
> . . I cannot describe the person I fired at. At that distance I could only see a figure with a weapon.

The soldier was not interviewed by the R.U.C. until the following day, 10 July 1981 at 12.25 pm. At that time he had two Army advisers present.

The Inquest jury was told that there was no evidence that a gun had been fired in the garden. No firearm residue was found on Danny and no spent cartridges were found at the scene. Counsel for the Army said they accepted that no gun was fired from Barrett's garden and that Danny was not a gunman. A forensic scientist told the jury that it would not have been possible for 'Soldier A', using the S.U.I.T. sight on his rifle, to see whether a person in Havana Court was carrying a firearm.

The jury's findings were as follows:

> A hunger-striker died in the Maze Prison on 8 July 1981 and there was rioting in the Ardoyne area of Belfast at times on that day and on the 9 July, during which shots were fired and petrol bombs thrown at the security forces. At about 9.35 pm a police Landrover drove along Flax Street and as it turned right into Ardoyne Avenue shots were fired from the junction of Brompton Park and Havana Court. These were observed through the S.U.I.T. sight attached to his rifle by a soldier stationed at an Observation Post on the roof of Flax Street Mill. He returned one shot which struck the deceased who was sitting on a low wall which separates his home from 12 Havana Court and caused his rapid death. The deceased was not a gunman or a rioter.

Current Status: Michael Meacher, a member of the British House of Commons, has referred the case to the Attorney-General, requesting that a prosecution should be brought against 'Soldier A'. At the time of our Inquiry no response had been received to this request.

The Barrett family's solicitor, Pascal O'Hare, informed us that the family is bringing a civil action against the British Government.

68. Patrick Elliott

Date & Place: 27 December 1982. Outside fish and chip shop on the Andersonstown Road, Belfast.

Undisputed Facts: Patrick Pearse Elliott was shot dead by soldiers of the First Black Watch regiment as he came out from a fish and chip shop where he and an associate had stolen money from the till. Both men wore masks and had been drinking heavily – forensic reports on Elliott revealed 'a considerable amount of alcohol in the body.'

Information: The Inquiry heard evidence from the manageress of the fish and chip shop, Mrs Josephine McDonnell who described the two masked men coming into the shop. One jumped over the counter and fell. The other remained in the customer area and lined people up against the wall. In her statement at the Inquest she said:

I seen a soldier looking through the grill as these two fellas were heading for the door. The fellas run on out and all I heard was shooting. The shots were not all together and there was six or eight altogether. None of·these fellas had a gun or knife as far as I could see. The one who came over the counter had no gloves on and I saw he wasn't holding a gun or any other weapon when he fell over the counter.

Mrs McDonnell's daughter Kathleen also testified at the Inquest that she was working with her mother behind the counter when the men came into the shop:

The first one. . . came to the counter and shouted something at my mother and me but I couldn't make out what he was saying. I noticed his eyes which seemed very big and staring. Then the two of them left the shop and the three of us had just turned to each other when I heard shots. We all ducked down behind the counter until the shooting was over. I think there were about 5 or 6 shots. I did not see any guns produced but both of the fellows were very aggressive. They did not have anything in their hands. When they went out I did not hear any shouting before the shooting. It was quiet in the shop and I would have heard any shouting.

Only one civilian witness statement referred to hearing a shout before the shooting. All of the soldiers' statements assert that a warning was shouted to Elliott before he was shot.

We heard again from Gerard McGivern, a volunteer ambulance driver and male nurse who is also a member of Amnesty International. He stated that the soldiers definitely gave Elliott no warning. After the shooting, he tried to approach Elliott as he lay in the road, in order to render first aid if necessary. He was seized, had a rifle muzzle put to his throat and was placed under arrest despite explaining his qualifications. When placed in an R.U.C. vehicle, Mr McGivern said that the officer with him asked if the man on the ground was dead. Mr McGivern replied that he believed he was and the officer then said:

I'm glad. That's another Fenian bastard.

Although he had left his forwarding address on leaving Belfast, Mr McGivern was not invited to attend the Inquest. He now runs a business in London and flew to Belfast specially to testify to the Inquiry about the shooting of Patrick Elliott.

Elliott's parents told us that two army officers came to their door that night after the shooting and asked a number of sarcastic questions about their son. At that time the family had not heard of his death and·the officers left without telling them.

Official Explanation: The Army stated that Elliott was armed with what appeared to be a pistol but turned out to be a small kitchen knife. An R.U.C. officer reported finding such a knife at the scene. The R.U.C. issued a statement that Elliott was wanted for the attempted murder of an R.U.C. man and for 30 armed robberies.

The family accept that Patrick Elliott had a bad record for a number of petty thefts. However, they are adamant that he was not involved with guns for any purposes. We have seen no evidence to suggest that Elliott had any paramilitary connections and the R.U.C. have given no explanation why they never visited the family to try and interview them or their son about the serious charges on which they claimed he was wanted.

Official Action: On 24 June 1983, six months after the death, the D.P.P. announced that there would be no prosecution. The family say they were not informed of this until 6 July, which was the first official notification they had received concerning their son's death. The Inquest took place on 2 September 1983 and statements of 'Soldiers A, B, C and D' were read.

The Jury's findings were as follows:

> At about 11.45 pm on 27 December 1982 two masked men entered The Red Barn Barbecue, a fish and chip shop at 127 Andersonstown Road, Belfast. They lined the customers up along a wall, jumped over the counter and took the money in the till. A passing Army patrol of four soldiers saw through the window what was happening. The masked men ran out of the shop. At this the Corporal in charge shouted: 'Army, Halt or Stop' or words to that effect. A masked man then turned and was shot by two soldiers and fell to the ground. The man could have moved while on the ground and was shot once on the ground. The only weapon carried by the deceased was a knife. The deceased was struck by four bullets which caused his rapid death. The other masked man was also fired at, but made good his escape. The concentration of alcohol in the blood of the deceased was 217 mg. per 100 ml.

Current Status: No further action has been reported.

69. *Maura Meehan and Dorothy McGuire*

Date & Place: 23 October 1971. West Belfast.

Undisputed Facts: Both were shot dead by the British Army as they were travelling in a car through the streets of West Belfast. The car was sounding its horn to warn of the presence of British troops in the area.

Information: The Inquiry heard evidence from Mrs Margaret Murray, Mrs Meehan's sister-in-law, who stated that after the shootings, the Army put out three successive statements claiming first, that the two were dressed as terrorists and had thrown two nail bombs from the car; secondly, that one nail bomb had been thrown; finally, that the army had been fired on from the car. At the Inquest a forensic expert stated that there were no traces of guns or bombs having been in the car. Neither woman was wearing what could possibly be described as paramilitary clothing.

Official Action: There were no prosecutions.

Current Status: After 12 years, Mrs Meehan's widower received a settlement of his claim against the British Army. The amount received was £1,200.

Notes

1. Statement of His Eminence, Cardinal Tomás Ó Fiaich, Archbishop of Armagh at the Funeral of Martin Malone on 1 August 1983.
2. Evidence of Mr. Joseph Rice, Solicitor, to the Inquiry.
3. *Sunday Times*, London, 8 April 1984.
4. *Sunday Press*, Dublin, 8 April 1984.
5. *New Statesman*, London, 15 June 1984.
6. *Sunday Press*, Dublin, 8 April 1984.
7. *Fortnight*, Belfast, September, 1984.
8. *Fortnight*, Belfast, October, 1984.
9. Ibid.
10. *Irish Times*, Dublin, 6 June 1984.
11. *Irish News*, Belfast, 5 June 1984.
12. Ibid.
13. *The Times*, London, 12 June 1984.
14. *Irish Times*, Dublin, 23 August 1984.
15. *Fortnight*, Belfast, September 1984.
16. *Irish Times*, Dublin, 11 June 1984.
17. Boyle K., Hadden T., Greer S.C., Walsh D., *Submission to the Review of the Northern Ireland (Emergency Provisions) Act 1978*, conducted by the Rt Hon. Sir George Baker OBE, 1983.
18. *The Events on Sunday 30th January 1972 which led to Loss of Life in Connection with the Procession in Londonderry on that Day*, H.C. 220 HMSO London, April 1972. See above, para. 34.
19. See above, para. 34.
20. *Belfast Telegraph*, 26 April 1984.
21. *Irish News*, 27 April 1984.
22. *Irish News*, 26 August 1982.
23. *Irish News*, 1 June 1983.
24. See above, paras. 37-38, for the killing of 12 year old Kevin Heatley by Corporal Foxford.

5. Plastic Bullets

70. At the time of our Inquiry's hearings, 11 people had been killed by this supposedly non-lethal riot control weapon. A number of unofficial inquiries had already reported on the plastic bullet's dangers. We were, of course, aware that the European Parliament had condemned these weapons[1] and that, as Home Secretary at the time of serious civil unrest in many parts of Britain in 1981, the then Home Secretary, Mr William Whitelaw, had reportedly refused to allow the British police to use plastic bullets because their use would 'mean inflicting injury or even death on rioters'.[2]

71. Since 1981, when eight people (four of them children) died from plastic bullet injuries, a number of hearings have been held in the North of Ireland and elsewhere and considerable international concern has been generated.[3]

Father Raymond Murray and Father Denis Faul supplied us with extensive documentation on plastic bullet killings.[4]

However, as we were preparing our report on the legal implications of the use of plastic bullets, we received details of the death of yet another victim, John Downes, 22 years old. We set out below a brief summary of the events leading to that death.

72. On 12 August 1984 a rally was held outside Sinn Féin headquarters in West Belfast to commemorate the thirteenth anniversary of the re-introduction of internment (see paras. 27-28 above). Martin Galvin, a New York attorney and spokesperson for Sinn Féin's United States support organisation, Irish Northern Aid, appeared on the platform to address the crowd. He had entered Northern Ireland in defiance of an exclusion order imposed by the then Secretary of State, Mr James Prior. As he was about to speak a large force of R.U.C. moved in.

73. Reporting for *The Times* of London, Richard Ford wrote:

Mr Galvin was greeted with wild cheering and had just finished waving to the crowd when the police moved in from both ends. They fired plastic bullets into the air and at almost point-blank range into the crowd as they ran over to the crowd, pulling them out of the way and then began driving landrovers into the screaming and hysterical people.

Appeals for calm went unheard as plastic bullets whirled around. People cowered on the road, clutching children and trying to cover their heads.[5]

Paul Johnson, of *The Guardian*, reported:

One man died and up to 20 people were injured, four seriously, yesterday, when Belfast police moved into a 3,000-strong crowd, flailing batons and firing plastic bullets with wanton disregard in an effort to capture Mr Martin Galvin . . .

As the police moved in, they acted with indiscriminate brutality towards the crowd. Those who tried to flee in panic or simply cowered on the pavement, were batoned. Plastic bullets were fired from close range, and at specific targets, in contravention of the rules governing their use.[6]

74. Strong criticisms of the R.U.C.'s actions and calls for an independent public inquiry came from many political figures in Britain, including Neil Kinnock, leader of Britain's Labour Party; David Steel, leader of the Liberal Party and Shirley Williams, president of the Social Democratic Party. Once again, the weapon's lethal impact requires lawyers to ask whether the plastic bullet conforms to international and domestic legal standards.

75. In 1983 the International League for Human Rights raised the issue of plastic bullets in Northern Ireland before the United Nations Sub-Commission on Prevention of Discrimination and Protection of Minorities. (See Appendix D, below). This caused the British Government to submit a written response in August 1983. The League points out that:

All 11 people killed have been Catholics. Inquests held in 1982 and 1983 have found that six of them were not involved in any disturbance which was going on at the time. The adjourned inquest into the death of Mrs Nora McCabe, the mother of two children, is almost certain to come to a similar finding. Thirty year-old Mrs Nora McCabe was shot by the Royal Ulster Constabulary from just six feet away.[7]

The British Government responded to the International League's criticisms on 29 August 1983 by denying the plastic bullets were ever employed unless absolutely necessary and in the course of a riot. They claimed that all incidents in which persons are killed or injured are fully investigated, reports sent to the Director of Public Prosecutions and complaints monitored by the Police Complaints Board. They also maintained that the use of plastic bullets is strictly monitored to ensure that official instructions are obeyed.[7a]

76. The Northern Catholic Bishops issued a statement entitled 'Ban Plastic Bullets' on Monday 4 July 1983. It stated, in part:

> Many people have been killed by these weapons, some of them very young. Each of these deaths has caused deep grief in the family of the victim. The deaths have generated resentment throughout whole communities and have been the cause of growing alienation among wide sections of the population. The most recent inquest on such a victim, a boy of 11 years old, made the following findings:
>
> (1) . . . there was insufficient evidence to suggest that Stephen McConomy was rioting when he was shot.
>
> (2) . . . he was shot from a range of 17 feet when the minimum recommended range is 60 feet.
>
> (3) . . . the riot gun from which the plastic bullet was fired was faulty.
>
> Rioting is morally wrong but the methods used to control it must also be subject to the moral law. There cannot be one law for the security forces and another for the public. The use of plastic bullets is morally indefensible. The plastic bullet should be withdrawn as a riot control weapon.

77. The Inquiry received evidence that the following have been killed by rubber and plastic bullets since 1969:

Killed	Age	Date	Place
Francis Rowntree*	11	20 Apr 1972	Divis Flats, Belfast
Tobias Molloy*	18	16 Jul 1972	Strabane
Thomas Friel*	21	17 May 1973	Derry City
Stephen Geddis	10	28 Aug 1975	Divis Flats, Belfast
Brian Stewart	13	4 Oct 1976	West Belfast
Michael Donnelly	21	10 Aug 1980	Ballymurphy
Paul Whitters	15	15 Apr 1981	Derry City
Julie Livingstone	14	12 May 1981	West Belfast
Carol Ann Kelly	12	19 May 1981	West Belfast
Henry Duffy	45	22 May 1981	Derry City
Nora McCabe	30	8 Jul 1981	West Belfast
Peter Doherty	33	24 Jul 1981	West Belfast
Peter McGuinness	41	9 Aug 1981	North Belfast
Stephen McConomy	11	16 Apr 1981	Derry City
John Downes	22	12 Aug 1984	West Belfast

* Denotes Rubber Bullets. N.B.: dates given are dates of injury, death frequently occurred some days later.

78. We received many complaints that plastic bullets were fired at point-blank or extremely close range, aimed at the head or upper body and fired indiscriminately at crowds. We reproduce below the British Army's rules on the use of plastic bullets as of Summer 1980:

Rules for Engagement for PVC Baton Rounds (Plastic Bullets)

General

1. Baton rounds may be used to disperse a crowd whenever it is judged to be minimum and reasonable force in the circumstances.

2. The rounds must be fired at selected persons and not indiscriminately at the crowd. They should be aimed so that they strike the lower part of the target's body directly (ie without bouncing).

3. The authority to use these rounds is delegated to the commander on the spot.

Additional Rules for the 25 Grain PVC Baton Round

4. Rounds must not be fired at a range of less than 20 metres except when the safety of soldiers or others is seriously threatened.

5. The baton round was designed and produced to disperse crowds. It can also be used to prevent an escape from HM Prisons if it is, in the circumstances, still considered to constitute the use of minimum and reasonable force. If a prisoner can be apprehended by hand, the baton must not be used.[8]

From the evidence it appears that all of these rules have been violated in a frequent and systematic fashion, suggesting that the official policy does not operate in practice. No single prosecution has resulted from these deaths despite this evidence.

79. The use of plastic bullets had declined drastically between 1981 and the first half of 1984. The British Government seemed at the time of our hearings to be sensitive to international opinion on this question. However, as both the death of John Downes and the Government's answers to the United Nations Sub-Commission on Prevention of Discrimination and Protection of Minorities indicate, use of the weapon will continue in Northern Ireland and potentially

in the rest of the United Kingdom in times of serious street disorders.

80. Because of its capacity to inflict serious injury and death, we have concluded that the plastic bullet cannot be lawfully used for riot control. We therefore agree with the European Parliament's resolution calling for the banning of plastic bullets from Northern Ireland and all parts of the European Community. As we discuss in the following section of our report, the Criminal Law Act (Northern Ireland) 1967 does not permit the use of greater force than is reasonable for self-defence. Article 2 of the European Convention on Human Rights does not allow the use of deadly force unless absolutely necessary in clearly defined circumstances.

All of the evidence we have received demonstrates that the plastic bullet is a lethal weapon which is therefore not suited to its avowed function of riot-control. We are further persuaded that this weapon has been used frequently in violation of the rules cited in para. 78 above, that it has been aimed at the upper body and head and that it has been fired at point-blank or close range far less than 20 metres.

Given the overwhelming evidence for banning the plastic bullet, we are especially disturbed at reports that the British Government is planning their more extensive use. According to *Fortnight*, the independent review from Northern Ireland, on 13 September 1984:

> During a European Parliament debate on plastic bullets, John Hume claimed that the British Government was developing a new rapid-fire plastic bullet gun. The British Ministry of Defence admitted that a weapon called 'Arwen' was undergoing ballistic tests.[9]

In our opinion, such tests should cease immediately and the plastic bullet should be withdrawn from use forthwith.

Notes

1. Faul D., Murray R., *Plastic Bullets – Plastic Government*, Belfast, October 1982. They record that on 13 May 1982 the European Parliament voted (110 votes to 43) to ban the use of plastic bullets throughout the European Economic Community.

2. *Irish News*, 6 August 1981, Editorial: As Mr John Hume said just three weeks ago: Nothing could underline our colonial status here in Northern Ireland more callously and blatantly than the refusal of the British Home Secretary, Mr William Whitelaw, to sanction the use of plastic bullets against British rioters after the savage outbreaks of violence in the Toxteth area of Liverpool and in other British cities. They must not be used, said the Home Secretary, because their use would 'mean inflicting injury or even death on rioters' . . . Just why is the Liverpool heaver of paving stones or Molotov cocktails more privileged than his opposite number in Northern Ireland? The answer is, of course, the one supplied by Mr Hume. We are the lesser breed without the law; or, in other words, there are no votes in Northern

Ireland and no one cares. However, Mr Whitelaw subsequently retracted his refusal to employ plastic bullets in Britain, saying in a written reply to the House of Commons on 25 February 1982: 'Some 3,000 baton rounds and 1,000 CS projectiles of approved types are now held by police forces in England and Wales for anti-riot purposes'.

3. *International Tribunal of Inquiry into Deaths and Serious Injuries caused by Rubber and Plastic Bullets*, 3/4 August 1981. *Second International Tribunal*, 1 October 1982. Gifford A., *Death on the Streets of Derry*, Report of Inquiry into deaths of Stephen McConomy, Gary English and Jim Brown, 1983.

4. See list at Appendix C.

5. *The Times*, London, 13 August 1984.

6. *The Guardian*, London, 13 August 1984.

7. International League for Human Rights, *Comments on the U.K. Government's response, 29 August 1983, to International League's intervention under Agenda Item 9 concerning restraints in the use of force by law enforcement officials.* (See below, Appendix E).

7a. Ibid.

8. Reproduced from Faul D., Murray R., *Rubber & Plastic Bullets Kill & Maim*, Belfast, August 1981.

9. *Fortnight*, October 1984.

6. Analysis of Evidence
in the light of
International and Domestic Law

81. The Inquiry's terms of reference obliged us to have regard to international and British domestic law affecting the lethal use of firearms by the security forces in Northern Ireland, and to examine, *inter alia*:

> 1. The official instructions for the use of firearms by the security forces.

Therefore we examined the extent to which international law imposes obligations on the Government and Courts of the United Kingdom. We reviewed the applicable domestic statutes and common law and analysed the leading judicial decisions on the use of firearms by the security forces to see whether these accord with Britain's obligations at the level of international law.

82. After careful consideration, we have concluded that:

(a) International law imposes binding obligations on the British Government to protect everyone's right to life and to ensure that its security forces use no more force than absolutely necessary in carrying out their duties;

(b) The domestic law of the United Kingdom fails to provide adequate protection of everyone's right to life;

(c) The security forces in Northern Ireland have, in many instances which were examined by the Inquiry, used more force than absolutely necessary in carrying out their duties;

(d) The judiciary in Northern Ireland and Britain have further weakened the force of domestic law by failing to interpret the relevant acts of Parliament in accordance with either common law or international law;

(e) Certain judges have effectively endorsed a form of quasi-martial law in Northern Ireland; and

(f) Internal army and police force instructions on the use of firearms are kept secret from the public and breaches of those instructions have gone unpunished.

These conclusions flow from the following analysis of the law and cases examined by the Inquiry.

International Law

83. The two relevant sources of treaty law on the right to life are the United Nations International Covenant on Civil and Political Rights (The Covenant) and the European Convention for the Protection of Human Rights and Fundamental Freedoms (The Convention).

We set out below the provisions which govern the United Kingdom's obligations to protect the right to life.

The United Nations International Covenant on Civil and Political Rights

84. Article 6 (1) of the Covenant, which has been ratified by the United Kingdom, provides:

> Every human being has the inherent right to life. This right shall be protected by law. No one shall be arbitrarily deprived of his life.

As the United Nations Human Rights Committee observed in its 1982 decision concerning Colombia:

> The right enshrined in this article is the supreme right of the human being. It follows that the deprivation of life by the authorities of the State is a matter of the utmost gravity. . . The requirements that the right shall be protected by law and that no one shall be arbitrarily deprived of his life mean that the law must strictly control and limit the circumstances in which a person may be deprived of his life by the authorities of the State.[1] (Emphasis added).

The U.N. Human Rights Committee's detailed findings in the Colombian case show how article 6 (1) should be applied. The Committee condemned the actions of security forces which resulted in arbitrary deprivation of life. They also found that: 'the right to life was not adequately protected by the law of Colombia'. This case is of great importance to the law and the actions of the security forces in Northern Ireland and we refer readers to page 78 *(Footnote 1)* for fuller details of the background to that case.

The European Covention for the Protection of Human Rights and Fundamental Freedoms

85. The British Government has also ratified the European Convention, which provides in Article 2 that:

> 1. Everyone's right to life shall be protected by law. No one shall be deprived of his life intentionally save in the execution of a sentence of a court following his conviction of a crime for which this penalty is provided by law.
> 2. Deprivation of life shall not be regarded as inflicted in contravention of this Article when it results from the use of force which is *no more than absolutely necessary*:
>> (a) in defence of any person from unlawful violence;
>> (b) in order to effect a lawful arrest or to prevent the escape of a person lawfully detained;
>> (c) in action lawfully taken for the purposes of quelling a riot or insurrection. (Emphasis added).

86. Article 15 of the Convention recognises that: 'In time of war or other public emergency threatening the life of the nation. . .' States may face crises which would justify derogation from certain rights guaranteed by the Convention. However, the right to life is regarded as inviolable under the Convention and Article 15 provides further that no party may derogate from it: '. . . except in respect of deaths resulting from lawful acts of war.'

87. Under Article 13, ratifying states also undertake to provide remedies for any breach of the right to life:

> Everyone whose rights and freedoms as set forth in this Convention are violated shall have an effective remedy before a national authority *notwithstanding that the violation has been committed by persons acting in an official capacity.* (Emphasis added).

88. At the time of our Inquiry the British Government had filed derogations under Article 15 of the Convention (and from the corresponding Article 4 of the International Covenant), asserting the following grounds:

> . . . the existence of organised terrorism and violent civil disturbance
> constituting a public emergency in Northern Ireland and of the exercise
> therein of certain emergency powers.[2]

But in October 1984 these notices of derogation were withdrawn.
The British Government, therefore, considers that the emergency
laws currently in force in Northern Ireland are now compatible, as
they stand, with the spirit and letter of the Convention and the
Covenant. The obligations deriving from these treaties are, con-
sequently, much stricter now than those which applied as a result
of the derogation. At the time of the Inquiry, the British Government
acknowledged that there was in Northern Ireland a 'public
emergency threatening the life of the nation'. Britain was therefore
strictly bound to ensure that deprivation of life resulted only from
'force which was no more than absolutely necessary'. We note that
the Government's official position thus ruled out 'lawful acts of war'
as a possible justification for killings by the security forces.

89. British courts have traditionally asserted that the rules of international law are part of domestic law. The leading textbook on the
subject of statutory interpretation, Maxwell's *Interpretation of
Statutes*, states:

> . . . every statute is to be interpreted, so far as its language permits, so
> as not to be inconsistent with. . . the established rules of international
> law, and the court will avoid a construction which would give rise to
> such inconsistency unless compelled to adopt it by plain and unambigu-
> ous language.[3]

In a number of cases, British and Northern Ireland courts have
interpreted statutes in such a way as not to conflict with Britain's
obligations under international law. The most notable one from
Northern Ireland is the judgment of Lord Chief Justice Lowry in *R.
v. Deery* (1975).

It is further arguable that the provisions of those treaties relating
to the right to life are declaratory of customary international law.
For the above reasons we are satisfied that British law requires the
courts to interpret all statutes in a manner consistent with the Covenant and Convention. Only 'plain and unambiguous language' can
compel the courts to adopt a different interpretation.

Domestic Law

90. Having reached this conclusion, we therefore examined British domestic law to find out whether under the customary common law or under any Act of Parliament there is any 'plain and unambiguous' language which conflicts with international law standards on the right to life. We will look first at the common law and then at the statutory modifications made by the 1967 Criminal Law Act.

91. Before 1967 the common law required an 'apparent necessity' before an 'officer of justice' might use deadly force:

> Where an officer of justice is resisted in the legal execution of his duty..., he may repel force by force; and if, in doing so, he kill the party resisting him, it is justifiable homicide...
>
> ... Still, *there must be an apparent necessity for the killing; for if the officer were to kill after the resistance had ceased,* [2 East P.C., 297], *or if there were no reasonable necessity for the violence used upon the part of the officer, etc. (R. v. Goffe,* 1 Vent. 216), *the killing would be manslaughter at the least.*[4]

Stephen's *New Commentaries on the Laws of England* also emphasise that:

> In all cases, *there must be an apparent necessity*; that is, it must be shown, e.g., that the party could not be otherwise secured, or that the riot could not be otherwise suppressed, or that the prisoners could not be otherwise kept in hold. For, *without such absolute necessity, the homicide is not justifiable.*[5]

92. Therefore, until the 1967 Criminal Law Act, British common law was broadly identical to Article 2 of the European Convention. 'Absolute necessity' or 'apparent necessity' were needed to justify any killing by the security forces. British lawyers helped to write the European Convention and when, in 1954, the British Government signed it, we believe it did so in good faith, believing British law to be consistent with its Articles.

93. However, the Criminal Law Act (Northern Ireland) 1967, Section 3(1) states:

> A person may use *such force as is reasonable in the circumstances* in the prevention of crime, or in effecting or assisting in the lawful arrest of offenders or suspected offenders or of persons unlawfully at large. (Emphasis added).

Identical provisions apply throughout the United Kingdom. This Act was passed before the British Army's deployment in Northern Ireland in 1969 and we agree with Professor D. S. Greer of the Law Faculty, Queen's University, Belfast, that:

> While section 3(1) of that Act may suffice for 'ordinary' conditions in England and Wales, the extraordinary conditions in Northern Ireland surely require more precision in the law relating to the use of deadly force.[6]

There is no statutory definition of the circumstances in which deadly force may be used by the security forces or by any other persons. This caused a leading authority on the powers of the security forces to write:

> It seems a pity that when the law was changed the legislation did not elucidate criteria governing the use of deadly force.[7]

94. The need for greater clarity about the power of the police to use deadly force has emerged recently in the *Waldorf* case in London (see below, para. 123). That need had, however, been all too clear in Northern Ireland for much longer, since, as Lord Chief Justice Lowry observed in 1975:

> The security forces are often operating in conditions with which the ordinary law was not designed to cope, and in regard to which there are no legal precedents.[8]

95. Before examining the decisions of judges in Northern Ireland and the rest of the United Kingdom arising under Section 3 (1) of the Criminal Law Act (Northern Ireland) 1967, we turned again to Maxwell's *Interpretation of Statutes*, (see above, para. 89) to see what rules the courts follow where there is a possible conflict between the common law and a new statute. In such cases there is a presumption against change in the common law:

> *Few principles of statutory interpretation are applied as frequently as the presumption against alterations in the common law.* It is presumed that the legislature does not intend to make any change in the existing law beyond that which is expressly stated in, or follows by necessary implication from, the language of the statute in question. It is thought to be *in the highest degree improbable that Parliament would depart from the general system of law without expressing its intention with irresistible clearness.*[9] (Emphasis added).

96. In other words, when Parliament used the words: 'such force as is reasonable in the circumstances', the courts should ask whether it was expressing with irresisitible clearness an intention to depart from the general system of law, i.e. the doctrine of 'apparent necessity'.

Indeed, since the courts also presume that statutes are intended to be consistent with the established rules of international law, we believe the courts should also ask whether the 1967 statute contained such 'plain and unambiguous language' as would compel the Courts to reject the requirement of 'absolute necessity' under the Convention and, more recently, under the Covenant.

97. However, we found no case in which a court in Northern Ireland or the United Kingdom had adopted these traditional approaches to statutory interpretation when dealing with Section 3 (1) of the Act.

In the sections of the Report which follow we review the leading cases and conclude that the wording of Section 3 (1) is so vague and ambiguous that it does not provide any legitimate grounds for departing from the principles of international and common law. These cases show that plain and unambiguous language is indeed required in order to bring the law in Britain and Northern Ireland within the ambit of international law.

The 'Yellow Card': Internal Instructions on the Use of Firearms by the Security Forces

98. Under our Terms of Reference we examined the internal instructions on the use of firearms by the security forces. However, since the British Army and R.U.C. refuse to provide copies of these instructions to members of the public we had to rely on other public documents. In this regard we agree with the Northern Ireland Standing Advisory Commission on Human Rights, which, in its report published in February 1984 (see Appendix E, below), stated:

> . . . we feel that the circumstances in which the security forces may open fire should be a matter of greater public knowledge and of public debate. If the circumstances in which the security forces are authorised to open fire were more widely known, there might be less danger of persons' lives being put at risk.[10]

99. The Army 'Yellow Card' as it is popularly known, has been considered in a number of court cases and it was a prosecution exhibit in the case of *R. v. Bailey and Jones*, (1983) 8 September,

Belfast Crown Court, Gibson L.J. We were shown a copy of that exhibit, which is dated November 1980. We believe that the public interest demands its publication here. We also reprint, for the purposes of comparison, the 'Yellow Card' marked 'revised 1972' which was supplied by another witness.

We note that the 1980 card, which applied at least as recently as August 1982, contains six paragraphs, by comparison with the 21 separate instructions in 1972. While the earlier card was criticised by Mr Justice MacDermott (see *R.* v. *Jones* below, para. 105) as 'to say the least, a difficult document', the 1980 card may appear by contrast as over-simplified:

The 1972 Yellow Card

RESTRICTED
Army Code No. 70771

*Instructions by the Director of Operations
for Opening Fire in Northern Ireland*

1. These instructions are for the guidance of Commanders and troops operating collectively or individually. When troops are operating collectively soldiers will only open fire when ordered to do so by the Commander on the spot.

General Rules
2. Never use more force than the minimum necessary to enable you to carry out your duties.
3. Always first try to handle the situation by other means than opening fire. If you have to fire:
    a. Fire only aimed shots.
    b. Do not fire more rounds than absolutely necessary to achieve your aim.
4. Your magazine/belt must always be loaded with live ammunition and be fitted to the weapon. Unless you are about to open fire no live round is to be carried in the breech and the working parts must be forward. Company Commanders and above may, when circumstances in their opinion warrant such action, order weapons to be cocked, with a round in the breech where appropriate, and the safety catch at safe.
5. Automatic fire may be used against identified targets in the same circumstances as single shots if, in the opinion of the Commander on the spot, it is the minimum force required and no other weapon can be employed as effectively. Because automatic fire scatters it is not to

---

be used where persons not using firearms are in, or may be close to, the line of fire.

Warning before firing

6. Whenever possible a warning should be given before you open fire. The only circumstances in which you may open fire without giving warning are described in paras. 13, 14 and 15 below.

7. A warning should be as loud as possible, preferably by loud hailer. It must:

    a. Give clear orders to stop attacking or to halt, as appropriate.

    b. State that fire will be opened if the orders are not obeyed.

You may fire after due warning

8. Against a person carrying what you can positively identify as a firearm,* but only if you have reason to think that he is about to use it for offensive purposes; he refuses to halt when called upon to do so, and there is no other way of stopping him.

9. Against a person throwing a petrol bomb if petrol bomb attacks continue in your area against troops and civilians or against property, if his action is likely to endanger life.

10. Against a person attacking or destroying property or stealing firearms or explosives, if his action is likely to endanger life.

11. Against a person who, though he is not a person attacking, has:

    a. in your sight killed or seriously injured a member of the security forces or a person whom it is your duty to protect and

    b. not halted when called upon to do so and cannot be arrested by any other means.

12. If there is no other way to protect yourself or those whom it is your duty to protect from the danger of being killed or seriously injured.

You may fire without warning

13. When hostile firing is taking place in your area and a warning is impracticable:

    a. Against a person using a firearm* against you or those whom it is your duty to protect

    b. against a person carrying what you can positively identify as a firearm* if he is clearly about to use it for offensive purposes.

14. At a vehicle if the occupants open fire or throw a bomb at you or those whom it is your duty to protect or are clearly about to do so.

15. If there is no other way to protect yourself or those whom it is your duty to protect from the danger of being killed or seriously injured.

Action by guards and at road blocks/checks

16. Where warnings are called for they should be in the form of specific challenges as set out in paragraphs 17 and 18.

17. If you have to challenge a person who is acting suspiciously you must do so in a firm, distinct voice, saying 'HALT – HANDS UP.'
    a. If he halts you are to say: 'STAND STILL AND KEEP YOUR HANDS UP.'
    b. Ask him why he is there, and if not satisfied call your Commander immediately and hand the person over to him.

18. If the person does not halt at once, you are to challenge again, saying 'HALT – HANDS UP' and, if the person does not halt on your second challenge, you are to cock your weapon, apply the safety catch and shout: 'STAND STILL I AM READY TO FIRE.'

19. The rules covering the circumstances for opening fire are described in paragraphs 8-14. If the circumstances do not justify opening fire, you will do all you can to stop and detain the person without opening fire.

20. At a road block/check, you will NOT fire on a vehicle simply because it refused to stop. If a vehicle does not halt at a road block/check, note its description, make, registration number and direction of travel.

21. In all circumstances where you have challenged and the response is not satisfactory you will summon your Commander at the first opportunity.

Revised November 1972.

NOTE: 'Firearm' includes a grenade, nail bomb or gelignite type bomb.

The 1980 Yellow Card

RESTRICTED
Army Code No. 70771

Instructions for Opening Fire in Northern Ireland

General Rules

1. In all situations you are to use the minimum force necessary. FIREARMS MUST ONLY BE USED AS A LAST RESORT.

2. Your weapon must always be made safe: that is, NO live round is to be carried in the breech and in the case of automatic weapons the working parts are to be forward, unless you are ordered to carry a live round in the breech or you are about to fire.

Challenging

3. A challenge MUST be given before opening fire unless:
    a. to do so would increase the risk of death or grave injury to you or any other person.

b. you or others in the immediate vicinity are being engaged by terrorists.

4. You are to challenge by shouting:

'ARMY: STOP OR I FIRE' or words to that effect.

Opening Fire

5. You may only open fire against a person:

a. if he* is committing or about to commit an act LIKELY TO ENDANGER LIFE AND THERE IS NO OTHER WAY TO PREVENT THE DANGER. The following are some examples of acts where life could be endangered, dependent always upon the circumstances:

(1) firing or being about to fire a weapon

(2) planting detonating or throwing an explosive device (including a petrol bomb)

(3) deliberately driving a vehicle at a person and there is no other way of stopping him*

b. if you know that he* has just killed or injured any person by such means and he* does not surrender if challenged and THERE IS NO OTHER WAY TO MAKE AN ARREST.

* 'She' can be read instead of 'he' if applicable.

6. If you have to open fire you should:

a. fire only aimed shots,

b. fire no more rounds than are necessary,

c. take all reasonable precautions not to injure any one other than your target.

100. The R.U.C. Press Office told one witness that their Force Instructions are in substantially the same terms as the 'Yellow Card' but refused to supply a copy. This contrasts with the London Metropolitan Police instructions which were made public by the British Home Secretary, who, following the shooting of Stephen Waldorf (see para. 123) told Parliament:

The Metropolitan Police rules governing the issue and use of firearms are rightly stringent and explicit. I am placing the relevant extracts from the current rules in the Library of the House. The rules say:

Every officer to whom a weapon is issued must be strictly warned that it is to be used *only in cases of absolute necessity*; for example, if he, or the person he is protecting is attacked by a person with a firearm or other deadly weapon *and he cannot otherwise reasonably protect himself or give protection, he may resort to firearms as a means of defence.*[11]

101. Beyond the mere wording of these instructions to the security forces, we looked to see what force they have at law. From the following judicial comments, the answer would appear to be that they have no force at all.

In *R. v. McNaughton*, [1975] N.I. 203, 206 Lord Chief Justice Lowry held that the 'Yellow Card' was:

> intended to lay down guidelines for the security forces but (did) not define the legal rights and obligations of members of the security forces under statute or common law. . . However, on reading the Yellow Card one may say that in some ways (the security forces) are intended. . . to be *more tightly restricted by the instructions they are given than by the ordinary law.* (Emphasis added).

As mentioned above, Lord Justice MacDermott criticised the document in *R. v. Jones* (1975) in Belfast Crown Court:

> For my part, I consider this card to be something which exists for some reason of policy and is intended to lay down guidelines to the forces but in my view it does not define the legal rights of the members of the security forces. No doubt it contains much sound advice, but I can readily understand that to many soldiers and perhaps others too, it is to say the least of it, a difficult document. The basic principles are that minimum force should be used and firing resorted to as a last resort. No one can gainsay the propriety and good sense of these propositions, but they must be considered in relation to the problem on the ground and though a man who acts dutifully in accordance with the Yellow Card might easily establish his conduct as being justifiable I do not accept that the failure to so act means *ipso facto* that his conduct is unlawful.

This judgment comes close to saying that the Yellow Card may well be a useful document in theory but that, in practice, soldiers cannot be expected to keep to it. A number of witnesses informed us that they consider the card a cosmetic device and that breaches of its instructions go unpunished as a matter of routine. Some confirmation of this view is found in a recent memoir of service in Northern Ireland by Captain A. F. N. Clarke, who served in the Third Parachute Regiment in Armagh at the time that regiment shot and killed Liam Prince (see above. para. 51):

> At least the same rules don't necessarily apply down here as they do in Belfast, or at least, *people are willing to turn a blind eye to any infringements of the letter of the yellow card.* Sure as hell, if I see some

bastard with a gun, I'm not about to ask him to surrender. Shoot first, then ask questions after. No way am I going to take any chances at all.[12]

102. Although the 'Yellow Card' and the Metropolitan Police Force Instructions seem broadly consistent with the letter of the International Covenant and the European Convention, we believe that the judges in Northern Ireland are not prepared to interpret these documents in that spirit. In view of the results of certain cases, notably that from which MacDermott J.'s remarks are taken, we conclude that members of the security forces must be aware, like Captain Clarke, that their superior officers and the judiciary will turn a blind eye to infringements of the instructions.

Notes

1. *Communication No. R.11/45.* Submitted by *Pedro Pablo Camargo* on behalf of the husband of *Maria Fanny Suarez de Guerrero: State party concerned: Colombia.*

Views of the Human Rights Committee adopted under Article 5 (4) of the Optional Protocol to the International Covenant on Civil and Political Rights. 31 March 1982.

The Committee found that the Colombian police acted under a Legislative Decree which purported to indemnify them for any penal act committed with the object of preventing extortion, kidnapping and drug trafficking. After searching a house for a kidnap victim, the police were unable to find him and lay in wait. The Committee held that Maria Fanny Suarez de Guerrero and six other 'innocent human beings' were:

> killed at point-blank range, some of them shot in the back or in the head. It was also established that the victims were not all killed at the same time, but at intervals as they arrived at the house, and that most of them had been shot while trying to save themselves from the unexpected attack.

The Supreme Court of Justice for Colombia had held the decree constitutional, stating:

> . . . this is a special measure that involves a right of social defence; for, on the one hand, it is legitimate that the members of the armed forces who are obliged to take part in operations like those described and whose purpose is to prevent or curb offences which, by their nature, are violent and are committed by means of violence against persons or property, should be protected by a justification of the punishable acts that they are constrained to commit, and, on the other hand, both the Government, acting on behalf of society, and society itself, have an interest in the defence of society and in ensuring that it is adequately defended by the agencies to which the law has entrusted the weapons for its defence.

The United Nations Human Rights Committee found that:

> In the present case it is evident from the fact that seven persons lost their lives as a result of the deliberate action of the police that the deprivation of life was intentional. Moreover, the police action was apparently taken without warning to the victims and without giving them any opportunity to surrender to the police patrol or to offer any explanation of their presence or intentions. There is no evidence that the action of the police was necessary in their own defence or that of others, or that it was necessary to effect the arrest or prevent the escape of the

persons concerned. Moreover, the victims were no more than suspects of the kidnapping which had occurred some days earlier and their killing by the police deprived them of all the protections of due process of law laid down by the Covenant. In the case of Mrs Maria Fanny Suarez de Guerrero, the forensic report showed that she had been shot several times after she had already died from a heart attack. There can be no reasonable doubt that her death was caused by the police patrol.

For these reasons it is the Committee's view that the action of the police resulting in the death of Mrs Maria Fanny Suarez de Guerrero was disproportionate to the requirements of law enforcement in the circumstances of the case and that she was arbitrarily deprived of her life contrary to article 6 (1) of the International Covenant on Civil and Political Rights. Inasmuch as the police action was made justifiable as a matter of Colombian law by Legislative Decree No. 0070 of 20 January 1978, the right to life was not adequately protected by the law of Colombia as required by article 6 (1). . .

. . . the Committee is accordingly of the view that the State party should take the necessary measures to compensate the husband of Mrs Maria Fanny Suarez de Guerrero for the death of his wife and to ensure that the right to life is duly protected by amending the law.

2. *Note Verbale*, from the Government of the United Kingdom to the Secretary-General of the Council of Europe, 18 December 1978. See also observations of Sir George Baker in his *Review of the Operation of the Northern Ireland (Emergency Provisions) Act 1978*, Cmnd. 9222, April 1984, para. 230:

The only member of the Council of Europe at present derogating from the Convention is Turkey. Under the Covenant, Chile, Uruguay, Colombia and Poland have derogated.

3. Maxwell, *Interpretation of Statutes*, (12th Edn. 1969), p. 183. Passage cited with approval in the House of Lords by Lord Simon of Glaisdale (dissenting) in *Cheng* v. *Governor of Pentonville Prison*, [1973] 2 All E.R. 204, 217.

4. Archbold, *Criminal Pleading, Evidence and Practice*, (35th Edn. 1962), pp. 1008-1009. (Emphasis added).

5. Stephen, *New Commentaries on the Laws of England*, (15th edition, 1908). Book VI, *Of Crimes*, pp. 39-40: 'Justifiable homicide committed for the advancement of public justice'. (Emphasis added).

6. Greer, D.S., 'Legal Control of Military Operations - A Missed Opportunity', 31 N.I.L.Q. 151.

7. Leigh, *Police Powers in England and Wales*, (1975), p.46. Cited in Greer, D.S., *op. cit.*

8. *R* v. *McNaughton* [1975] N.I. 203, 208.

9. Maxwell, *op. cit.*, p.116.

10. *Ninth Report of the Standing Advisory Commission on Human Rights* (NISACHR Report), HC 262, 1984. Para. 24.

11. H.C. Debates, 17 January 1983. (Emphasis added).

12. Clarke A.F.N., *Contact*, 1983, p. 98. (Emphasis added).

7. Judicial Authority on the Use of Firearms by the Security Forces

103. At the time our inquiry was held, a number of soldiers and police officers had been tried on charges of unlawful use of their firearms while on duty.[1] We learned that only one, Private Robert Reid Davidson, had been convicted of any such offence. He fired at a car passing through a border checkpoint at Strabane, killing a woman passenger and he was convicted of manslaughter. He received a 12 month sentence, suspended for two years.[2] Subsequently Private Ian Taine was sentenced to life imprisonment for the murder of Thomas O'Reilly (see above para. 41).

104. Apart from criminal prosecutions in the non-jury Diplock Courts, civil actions have been brought against the British Ministry of Defence. These have also resulted in rulings from senior judges on the circumstances in which the Army and R.U.C. may use deadly force. Two principal cases have been considered by the House of Lords, the highest court of appeal in the United Kingdom. *Attorney-General for Northern Ireland's Reference* [1977] A.C. 105 arose from a criminal prosecution, while the second case, *Farrell* v. *Ministry of Defence* [1980] 1 All E.R. 166, was a civil action for damages.

Since House of Lords decisions are binding on all civil and criminal courts throughout the United Kingdom, that court's interpretations of the Criminal Law Act (Northern Ireland) 1967, Section 3 (1), determine the rights and duties of the security forces under the Act. We have therefore examined these decisions in detail.

The Attorney-General's Reference

105. The details of the killing of *Patrick McElhone*, together with the trial and acquittal of Private Jones by Mr Justice MacDermott, are set out in our Evidence section above, at para. 53. This case turned on the judge's interpretation of 'such force as is reasonable in the circumstances' and MacDermott J. held that 'the circumstances' included:

(i) The 'general wartime situation' in Northern Ireland;
(ii) The actual particular problem facing the soldier on the ground – e.g. the character of the area;
(iii) Whether or not the accused suspected that the fugitive was an offender and whether, if he did, such a belief was reasonable, even though it may have been mistaken;
(iv) Whether the accused believed honestly and reasonably that it was his duty to open fire;
(v) Whether the alternatives were reasonably viable, given the accused's state of mind and the other circumstances.

106. The acquittal of Private Jones and the broad interpretation MacDermott J. gave to 'the circumstances' caused the Attorney-General to exercise his rarely used power to refer the case first to the Northern Ireland Court of Criminal Appeal and finally to the House of Lords for their opinion on the following point of law:

1. (i) Whether a soldier commits a crime when, in the circumstances set out in paragraph 2 below, he fires to kill or seriously wound an unarmed person because he honestly and reasonably believes that that person is a member of a proscribed organisation (in this case the Provisional I.R.A.) who is seeking to run away, and the soldier's shot kills that person;
(ii) whether, if a soldier commits a crime in killing a person at whom he shoots in the circumstances set out in question (i) . . . and in paragraph 2 . . . he is guilty of murder or manslaughter.

The facts as found by Mr Justice MacDermott were set out in paragraph 2 of the Reference:

(i) The accused, who was a soldier on duty, killed the deceased, who was a young man, with one shot from his S.L.R. rifle when the deceased was less than 20 yards from him in a field in a country area in daylight. The field was close to the farmhouse where the deceased lived with his parents and formed part of the farm.
(ii) The shot was a quick snap shot at the body of the deceased after the accused had shouted 'Halt' and the deceased had immediately run off. The shot was not preceded by a warning shot.
(iii) The deceased had not been under arrest at the time when the accused shouted 'Halt'. . .
(v) The said area was one in which troops had been attacked and killed by the I.R.A.; it was an area in which soldiers faced a real threat to their lives and where the element of surprise attack by the I.R.A. was a real threat. The said patrol had been briefed to expect attack and to be wary of being led into an ambush. The patrol was in an area which

the members of the patrol were entitled to regard as containing people
who might be actively hostile. . .

(viii) The deceased was unarmed and appeared to the accused to be
unarmed.

(ix) The deceased was alone and was not one of a number of persons
acting in a group.

(x) The accused was wearing full military equipment and pack. . .

(xii) The deceased was an entirely innocent person who was in no
way involved in terrorist activity.

(xiii) When the accused fired he honestly and reasonably believed that
he was dealing with a member of the Provisional I.R.A. who was seeking
to run away but he had no belief at all as to whether the deceased had
been involved in acts of terrorism or was likely to be involved in any
immediate act of terrorism. This being the state of mind of the accused
when he fired, he did so because he thought it was his duty so to do
and that firing was the reasonable and proper way to discharge his
duty in the circumstances.[3]

107. In the Northern Ireland Court of Appeal, Lord Chief Justice
Lowry and Lord Justice Jones upheld MacDermott J.:

(i) Since the respondent, Jones, honestly and reasonably believed that
the deceased was a member of the I.R.A. and since this is an offence
punishable with up to 5 years imprisonment (s.19 Northern Ireland
(Emergency Provisions) Act 1973) it is an arrestable offence within s.2
of the Criminal Law Act (Northern Ireland) 1967. Therefore, the defendant was entitled to arrest the deceased by virtue of s.12 of the 1973
Act and s.2 of the 1967 Act. He was also entitled to stop and question
him under s.16 of the 1973 Act.

(ii) The degree of force which is lawful to achieve these objectives is
the degree of force which is reasonable in the circumstances and this
is a matter to be decided by the tribunal of fact.[4]

Only Lord Justice McGonigal sounded a cautionary note, seeking
to limit the permissible use of deadly force:

In a case such as this, the trial judge should direct the tribunal of fact
that it is not reasonable for a soldier or policeman to fire with the
intention of killing or causing grievous bodily harm to an unarmed
man who is suspected of being a card-carrying member of the Provisional I.R.A. to prevent him from escaping answering further questions
even if the accused honestly considers it a reasonable discharge of his
duty to do so'.[5]

108. In the House of Lords, where Lord Diplock delivered the leading judgment, Lord Justice McGonigal's dissent was effectively overruled. The Lords followed the Court of Appeal in refusing to interfere with the trial judge's assessment of the facts. We believe it is important to look carefully at Lord Diplock's reasoning and his commentary on Northern Ireland affairs.

Lord Diplock ruled out any question of self-defence, holding that:

> The facts . . . are not capable in law of giving rise to a possible defence of 'self-defence'. The deceased was in fact, and appeared to the accused to be, unarmed. He was not attacking the accused: he was running away. So if the act of the accused in shooting the deceased was lawful it must have been on the ground that it was done in performance of his duty to prevent crime or in the exercise of his right to stop and question the deceased under section 12 of the Northern Ireland (Emergency Provisions) Act 1973.[6]

Lord Diplock continued:

> There is little authority in English law concerning the rights and duties of a member of the armed forces of the Crown when acting in aid of the civil power; and what little authority there is relates almost entirely to the duties of soldiers when troops are called upon to assist in controlling a riotous assembly. Where used for such temporary purposes it may not be inaccurate to describe the legal rights and duties of a soldier as being no more than those of an ordinary citizen in uniform. But such a description is in my view misleading in the circumstances in which the army is currently employed in aid of the civil power in Northern Ireland. In some parts of the province there has existed for some years now a state of armed and clandestinely organised insurrection against the lawful government of Her Majesty by persons seeking to gain political ends by violent means – that is, by committing murder and other crimes of violence against persons and property. Due to the efforts of the army and police to suppress it the insurrection has been sporadic in its manifestations but, as events have repeatedly shown, if vigilance is relaxed the violence erupts again.[7]

109. This assessment of the politico-military affairs of Northern Ireland is of profound legal significance. Lord Diplock rejects the concept of 'civilians in uniform' and describes the army's role in terms close to a state of siege, where martial law would rule. He goes on to amplify the difficult position in which a soldier in Northern Ireland is placed:

... under a duty, enforceable under military law, to search for criminals, if so ordered by his superior officer and to risk his own life should this be necessary in preventing terrorist acts. For the performance of this duty he is armed with a firearm, a self-loading rifle, from which a bullet, if it hits the human body, is almost certain to cause serious injury, if not death'.[8]

The armed soldier thus appears as the victim of circumstances equipped with a weapon so powerful that the natural consequence of firing must be death or serious injury. Since the law always presumes a person to intend the natural consequences of his actions, it is hard to understand Lord Diplock's observation that:

... it is only fair to the accused to mention that the trial judge was not satisfied that the accused when he fired the fatal shot did so with the intention of killing or seriously injuring the deceased.[9]

Finally, Lord Diplock extends his interpretation of 'the circumstances' for the purposes of Section 3 (1) of the 1967 Act to include not only the above political and military analysis but also to embrace the entire economic and social conditions of Northern Ireland. In reading his judgment, despite his frequent references to the role of the jury, it must be remembered that Private Jones was tried in a non-jury 'Diplock' Court. He writes that:

The jury would have to consider how the circumstances in which the accused had to make his decision whether or not to use force and the shortness of time available to him for reflection, might affect the judgment of a reasonable man. In the facts that are to be assumed for the purposes of the reference there is material upon which a jury might take the view that the accused had reasonable grounds for apprehension of imminent danger to himself and other members of the patrol if the deceased were allowed to get away and join armed fellow-members of the Provisional I.R.A. who might be lurking in the neighbourhood, and that the time available to the accused to make up his mind what to do was *so short that even a reasonable man could only act intuitively*. This being so, a jury ... should remind themselves that the postulated balancing of risk against risk, harm against harm, by the reasonable man is not undertaken in the calm analytical atmosphere of the courtroom after counsel with the benefit of hindsight have expounded at length the reasons for and against the kind and degree of force that was used by the accused; but in the brief second or two which the accused had to decide whether to shoot or not and under all the stresses to which he was exposed...

A reasonable man would know that a bullet from a self-loading rifle, if it hit a human being, at any rate at the range at which the accused fired, would be likely to kill him or to injure him seriously. So in one scale of the balance the harm to which the deceased would be exposed if the accused aimed to hit him was predictable and grave and the risk of its occurrence high. In the other scale of the balance it would be open to the jury to take the view that it would not be unreasonable to assess the kind of harm to be averted by preventing the accused's *(sic)* escape as even graver – the killing or wounding of members of the patrol by terrorists in ambush, and the *effect of this success by members of the Provisional I.R.A. in encouraging the continuance of the armed insurrection and all the misery and destruction of life and property that terrorist activity in Northern Ireland has entailed.* (Emphasis added). [10]

110. In parenthesis, it should be noted that the actual accused was Private Jones. The victim of his bullet – and of Lord Diplock's error – was Patrick McElhone, a young farmer who, the prosecution acknowledged, had no connection with any paramilitary organisation or activity (see above, para. 53).

111. At no stage in the House of Lords hearing was Britain's responsibility at international law raised. While the Attorney-General did make reference to the doctrine of 'necessity' under the common law, no member of the court addressed even that question. Thus, the *Attorney-General's Reference* failed to make any clearer what legal limitations control the use of deadly force by the army and police. Following this judgment and prior to our Inquiry, no member of the security forces had been found guilty of unlawful use of firearms while on duty.

112. We find that Lord Diplock's interpretation of 'the circumstances' cannot be justified by reference to Maxwell on *Interpretation of Statutes*, neither can such a departure from the common law as Lord Diplock clearly proposes by placing the security forces above the category of 'civilians in uniform'. The effect of this judgment is that a soldier or police officer need only tell a Diplock Court judge that he honestly and reasonably believed an innocent civilian to be a member of a paramilitary organisation and the judge will be bound, according to Lord Diplock, to accept that explanation. No immediate criminal action need be feared, merely the spectre of some form of success by a paramilitary group which would serve to increase the misery and destruction of life and property in the North of Ireland.

113. Based on our examination of the number of unjustifiable killings by members of the security forces and the comparatively

small number of prosecutions resulting from those killings, we
believe that Lord Diplock and his fellow House of Lords judges have
effectively discouraged the prosecuting authorities from bringing
members of the security forces to trial and simultaneously encouraged the belief that members of the security forces are above the law
or subject to different laws from those governing both the Nationalist
and Unionist communities in Northern Ireland.

The Farrell Case

114. The only other leading case in which the House of Lords has
ruled on the use of deadly force by the Army and R.U.C. in Northern
Ireland is the civil action brought by Mrs Farrell against the Ministry
of Defence. She claimed damages for negligence, assault and battery
against four soldiers who opened fire, killing her husband and two
other men as they fled after attempting an unarmed robbery in Newry
in 1971.

The facts, briefly stated, were that the three men, James
McLaughlin (Mrs Farrell's husband), Sean Ruddy and Robert
Anderson, had no connection with any paramilitary organisation or
activity. However, the Army had received information of a possible
bomb attack on a bank in Newry and four soldiers were stationed
at night on top of a building opposite the bank. Two men came to
the bank and while they were placing money in the night safe
McLaughlin, Ruddy and Anderson, who were unarmed, attempted
to rob them. The soldiers said they thought this was the bombing
raid and called on the men to stop. When they ran they were shot
dead.

115. Mrs Farrell's civil claim against the Ministry of Defence is
extremely important in showing how the courts consider the question
of reasonable force in a non-criminal matter. At first instance, the
trial judge withdrew the issue of negligence from the jury, leaving
them a series of questions on the allegations of assault and battery.
The jury found for the soldiers and Mrs Farrell appealed.

116. In the Northern Ireland Court of Appeal, Lord Chief Justice
Lowry, Lord Justice Jones and Lord Justice McGonigal ordered a
new trial on the ground *inter alia* that consideration should be given
to:

> the circumstances in which the operation was conceived and planned
> as well as those in which the decisive act was performed.

Lord Chief Justice Lowry held that:

> The nature of the security problem and the public importance of achieving success in its solution are relevant in setting the standard for the purpose of deciding whether, in a particular situation, the duty to take reasonable care has been observed.[11]

117. However, before a jury could retry the case, the Ministry of Defence appealed to the House of Lords which overturned the Court of Appeal decision. Having exhausted all her remedies in the United Kingdom, Mrs Farrell took her case to the European Commission of Human Rights in Strasbourg.

In December 1982, the Commission declared that Mrs Farrell's complaint of a breach of Article 2 of the Convention was admissible. At the time of our Inquiry, legal arguments had been submitted to the Commission but no final opinion had been delivered. Subsequently, it was reported that a 'friendly settlement' had been reached by the parties. This is a frequent practice of the Commission which, lacking enforcement powers to implement its opinions and those of the European Court, always encourages parties to settle disputes amicably where possible. The unfortunate corollary of such settlements is that the Commission refrains from issuing an official opinion on the legality of the practice complained of.

The House of Lords judgment therefore remains the last word on the British Government's civil liability for the killing of unarmed civilians by members of its security forces. We now turn to examine the House's approach to the *Farrell* case and the strong contrast their interpretation provides to the *Attorney-General's Reference*.

118. Lord Diplock was not sitting when the House of Lords heard the *Farrell* case. Instead of adopting his broad interpretation of 'the circumstances' from the *Attorney-General's Reference,* the House found that, in reviewing the potential liability of the Ministry of Defence for its agents' actions, 'the circumstances' must be construed narrowly. The House of Lords held that:

> [Section 3(1)] ... can only provide a defence for those who used force and if the force the four soldiers used was reasonable in the circumstances in which they used it, the defects, if there were any, in the planning of the operation would not deprive them of that defence and render the force used unreasonable . . .

Viscount Dilhorne observed that:

> . . . The question of negligence on the part of others could have been
> pleaded in the original statement of claim but it was not and *no useful
> purpose would be served by considering it in this appeal.* (Emphasis
> added).[12]

119. The contrast between the House of Lords ruling in *Farrell* and
that in *Attorney-General's Reference* could hardly be greater. Since
the House principally hears points of law of public importance, we
must assume that they heard the *Farrell* case for this reason. The
potential liability of the Ministry of Defence for the negligent planning or conduct of security force operations is a matter of the utmost
importance, especially in the context of Northern Ireland. We certainly cannot accept that 'no useful purpose would be served by
considering it'. The failure of Mrs Farrell's legal advisers to allege
negligence against the planners of the operation was thus used by
the House of Lords to avoid the real issue of public importance.

120. Professor D.S. Greer of the Faculty of Law, Queen's University,
Belfast has argued that the House of Lords:

> . . . missed a timely opportunity to clarify an area of law which has
> become unacceptably vague and uncertain. . .
>
> The House is well accustomed to fulfilling its role as declarer or
> developer of the law notwithstanding the fact that the particular case
> could be resolved on a narrow technical ground. *Farrell's* case raised
> a question of law of sufficient public importance to demand at least
> some observations on the relevant law. When one considers that the
> case is but one of a considerable line of recent cases in which the House
> has been asked – and generously responded – to develop the law of
> negligence, this omission is all the more indefensible.[13]

121. Professor Greer surmises that the House of Lords may have
shown reticence in this case due to:

> . . . an unwillingness to expose the four soldiers to possible prosecution
> for murder or manslaughter. On the face of it, this seems a reasonable
> consideration; if anyone is to be criminally responsible, should it not
> be the commanding officer who planned the operation? On reflection,
> however, such an approach may be seen as rather shortsighted. To give
> section 3 (1) the narrower meaning of 'circumstances' is to provide in
> effect a defence of 'superior orders'.[14]

In all the discussion of section 3 (1) the applicability of this criminal
statute to a civil law case seems to be taken for granted. However,
in the *Farrell* case the issue is not criminal but civil liability. It is the

right of a widow to damages from a Government ministry for the negligent acts and omissions of that ministry's agents. A criminal defendant is innocent until proved guilty beyond a reasonable doubt; whereas in a civil case, a person's bereaved spouse is, or should be, entitled to a legal presumption that it is *prima facie* unreasonable, and thus at least negligent, to kill in the absence of absolute necessity. Professor Greer rightly points out that, by defining 'the circumstances' so narrowly, the House of Lords is effectively giving the soldiers a defence of 'superior orders'. Any such defence was finally and incontestably rejected by the Nuremberg Tribunal on Nazi War Crimes and has no place in domestic or international law or, for that matter, in the British Army Manual. Both the planners and perpetrators of a crime are criminally responsible. They cannot hide behind 'superior orders' whether they be civilians or members of the security forces.

122. In addition to these House of Lords cases, three recent prosecutions of police officers – two Northern Ireland cases and one in London – have led to increased public concern and awareness about the use of firearms by the security forces. We therefore reviewed the shootings of Steven Waldorf, by Metropolitan Police Officers in London; Seamus Grew and Roddy Carroll, by an undercover unit of the R.U.C. in Armagh City; and Gervaise McKerr, Eugene Toman and Sean Burns, by the same R.U.C. unit in Lurgan.

The Case of Steven Waldorf

123. The brief facts were that, in September 1983, two London police officers were tried on charges of attempted murder and grievous bodily harm. They had been shadowing a vehicle which they mistakenly believed was driven by a dangerous wanted man. One officer drew his weapon in breach of force instructions. He said he thought the driver had bent forward as if reaching for a gun, so he fired, again in breach of instructions, to stop the car. He failed to shout a warning. A second officer fired several shots into the front of the car with the intent to kill or seriously wound the driver. Mr Waldorf fell out of the car, badly shot and bleeding. The officers then pistol-whipped him around the head, causing multiple skull fractures. They claimed that they still believed they were in danger.

124. Mr Justice Croom-Johnson directed the Old Bailey jury (there

being no Diplock Courts in England) that the issue was self-defence:
the officers should be judged on what they believed to be the facts,
namely that they were facing a dangerous criminal who was going
for his gun. The judge held that the circumstances in which force
might be reasonable were not limited to 'force instructions' and that
a breach of instructions would not make the officers guilty of a
criminal offence. (Cf. MacDermott J. in *R. v. Jones*, para. 53 above).
He told the jury that continued force after the shooting was also
justified if the officers still believed they were in danger.[15]

125. The jury acquitted the officers on all charges and we are aware
that considerable public concern has resulted from the judge's
instructions and from subsequent shootings by London officers
which have prompted the Greater London Council to establish an
Inquiry into the use of firearms by the Metropolitan Police. The
Haldane Society of Socialist Lawyers, in evidence to our Inquiry,
laid particular emphasis on the impact of this case, writing that:

> If this happens in the streets of London, at a time of no particular
> security alert, then it is difficult to envisage what protection the citizens
> of Northern Ireland can receive from the criminal law in similar circum-
> stances . . . Unless the words 'prevention of crime' are given a narrow
> judicial construction, *English law may permit the selective assassination
> of members of proscribed organisations, or anyone else believed to
> have participated in serious offences, by the security forces.* The
> supreme judicial body has twice refused to give any construction of
> these words. (Emphasis added).

The Killings of Seamus Grew and Roddy Carroll

126. R.U.C. Constable John Robinson was charged with the murder
of Grew and tried in April 1984 by Mr Justice MacDermott. The
details of these killings are set out at para. 54 above but here we are
concerned with the reasons Robinson gave for killing the two
unarmed men and the reasons MacDermott J. gave for acquitting
Robinson.

127. Constable Robinson testified that he was a member of 'E4A',
an undercover unit trained by the Special Air Service (S.A.S.) regiment of the British Army. Chris Ryder, a journalist with the London
Sunday Times, reported on Robinson's testimony as follows:

> One feature of the training is that *the traditional police concept of use
> of minimum force is abandoned.* In one exercise, officers have to burst
> into what is known as the *'killing room'* and fire a set number of shots

into a dummy within a certain time. The exercise, aimed at developing *'firepower, speed and aggression'*, is repeated until the officer meets the standard.[16]

The existence of these undercover police units, trained to use maximum, rather than minimum force, has been confirmed by a senior R.U.C. Deputy Chief Constable (para. 55 above).

128. According to the *Sunday Times*:

> The units are not unique to Northern Ireland; they were set up by a joint directive of the Home Office and the Association of (Chief) Police Officers that requires every chief constable to have a team of highly trained men who would handle incidents involving hostages, sieges and terrorists. This is part of the strategy of keeping the army out of internal security work in Britain.[17]

In early 1984 the British Parliament learned that in 1976 the then Home Secretary, without the knowledge of his Prime Minister, had armed London's Metropolitan Police with sub-machine guns. The secret establishment and training of these Special Branch units emerged at the same time, demonstrating how security measures, ostensibly designed for Northern Ireland, can also be implemented covertly in Britain.

129. We find that the British Government, in training special units in tactics outlawed by international law, is encouraging violations of the European Convention and of domestic law. Such tactics are aimed at placing the security forces either above the law altogether or, at the least, subjecting them to criteria far less stringent than those applied to the civilian population.

130. None of this evidence might have emerged if Mr Justice Mac-Dermott had granted Constable Robinson's motion to dismiss the charges at the end of the prosecution case. However, after his detailed testimony, according to Mary Holland, writing in the *New Statesman*:

> In court the trial judge praised Constable Robinson for his sharp shooting.[18]

This statement, in conjunction with Robinson's acquittal, has been perceived as a serious departure from the even-handed application of the rule of law and is tantamount to the unleashing of the security forces from the legal constraints under which they must operate. In the light of his observations, many reasonable people must consider that the administration of justice would be best served if MacDermott J. were to recuse himself from any cases brought under emergency legislation as public confidence in the judiciary has been impaired by MacDermott J.'s utterances in this case.

The Killings of Eugene Toman, Gervaise McKerr and Sean Burns

131. While we were preparing this Report, Sergeant William Montgomery, Constable David Brannigan and Constable Frederick Robinson were tried for the murder of Eugene Toman. Lord Justice Gibson, sitting in a Diplock Court, acquitted the three R.U.C. officers at the end of the prosecution case. (See para. 55 above for the details of these shootings).

132. The three officers were also members of the 'E4A' unit of the R.U.C. Special Branch. In describing their training, Deputy Chief Constable Michael McAtamney told Judge Gibson:

> 'Once you have decided to fire, you shoot to take out your enemy.'
> 'Do you mean, permanently out of action?' asked the judge.
> 'Yes,' replied Mr McAtamney.[19]

Mr McAtamney further confirmed the details of the unit's training which Constable John Robinson had testified to in the Grew case (see para. 127) and Lord Justice Gibson not only found the officers' actions reasonable in the circumstances but, having announced his intention of acquitting the accused he adjourned the case until the following day when he stated:

> I wish to make it clear that having heard the Crown case I regard each of the accused as absolutely blameless in this matter. That finding should be put in their record along with my own commendation for their courage and determination in *bringing the three deceased men to justice, in this case the final court of justice.*[20] (Emphasis added).

In what appears to be an attempt to boost the morale of the security forces as well as an attack on the role of the Attorney-General and the Director of Public Prosecutions, Lord Justice Gibson said:

> The case is going to have a more widespread effect among other members of the security forces generally. When a policeman or soldier is ordered to arrest a dangerous criminal and on the basis of that order to *bring him back dead or alive*, how is he to consider his conduct now?[21] (Emphasis added).

133. We are satisfied that there is no authority in the wording of Section 3 (1) of the Criminal Law Act (Northern Ireland) 1967 to justify any judge in using such expressions as 'the final court of justice' and 'bring him back dead or alive'. These unprecedented statements, made by Northern Ireland's second most senior judge, are without parallel. Both domestic and international law emphatically prohibit such an approach.

Ministers in the Irish Government immediately joined with moderate Nationalist representatives in the North in condemning these remarkable decisions. The Northern Ireland Criminal Bar (Solicitors) Association recommended that the judge should 'consider his position carefully'.[22]

134. The judgments of Lord Justice Gibson and of Mr Justice MacDermott in the *Robinson* case already considered, lead us to adopt the Haldane Society's criticisms of the present state of the law in the United Kingdom. We find that:

(i) the criminal law fails to indicate when deadly weapons may be used;
(ii) the right to use reasonable force afforded by Section 3 (1) of the 1967 act is an inappropriate formula when applied to lethal weapons in the lawful possession of the security forces;
(iii) the attempt to apply the same principles of criminal liability to ordinary members of the public and the security forces is defeated when the latter are equipped with deadly weapons and placed in circumstances when they may be under a duty to use them.

135. We believe that Lord Justice Gibson, through his own words, has amplified the inadequacy of this legislation and has subverted what ordinary members of the public may rightly consider to be legitimate constraints on the security forces. It is essential that all sections of the community in Northern Ireland should have the fullest confidence in the judicial process and the knowledge we have gained from the families of a number of those killed by the security forces forces us to the conclusion that Lord Justice Gibson should also recuse himself from all cases in the emergency legislation.

British Security Forces Operating inside the Irish Republic

136. While inquiring into the role of the security forces in Northern Ireland we learned of a number of armed operations organised by the British Army and R.U.C. within the Irish Republic. The United Nations Charter and customary international law expressly prohibit the violation of a state's territorial integrity and outlaw all armed interference by the forces of one state in the internal affairs of another.

137. During February 1984 the *New Statesman* magazine in Britain published three articles entitled: 'British Army "Dirty Tricks" in

Northern Ireland', in which a former Army intelligence officer named Fred Holroyd asserted that Army officers planned and paid for illegal kidnap operations in the Republic in 1974 and mudered an I.R.A. suspect there in 1975. Mr Noel Dorr, the Irish Ambassador to Britain was quoted as saying:

> It's simply not acceptable that there should be security forces of any other state operating within our jurisdiction.[23]

138. According to Captain Holroyd, the British Army recruited Jimmy O'Hara, a Lisburn Protestant and ex-boxer to kidnap Seamus Grew from the Irish Republic in March 1974. (See above, para. 54). The *New Statesman* reported that:

> Earlier this year, O'Hara confirmed to us that he and two friends had indeed been hired by an Army officer to kidnap Grew. The officer supplied detailed maps showing Grew's house, details of his movements, official surveillance photographs and a sketch plan to show them where to dump Grew in Northern Ireland after they had kidnapped him.[24]

139. During the trial of Constable Robinson for the murder of Seamus Grew the officer revealed that he and his undercover surveillance unit had followed Grew and Carroll to Monaghan in the Irish Republic. The Irish *Sunday Press* reported that:

> It was in answer to his own defence counsel that Constable Robinson dropped the 'out-of-the-blue' bombshell about the role of the Special Branch. 'I believe their involvement was that they were operating at that time outside our own jurisdiction,' he said.[25]

The *Irish Times*, on 9 April 1984, pointed out that Robinson's testimony had precedents in a number of incidents in 1976, chronicled by journalist Patsy McArdle, including the kidnapping from the Irish Republic of Sean McKenna, a leading Republican, by the S.A.S., as well as the murder there of Seamus Ludlow, who bore a strong resemblance to a leading I.R.A. man then on the run in the South.[26]

140. The Chief Constable of the R.U.C., Sir John Hermon, claimed in response to protests from the Republic and Britain that:

> There was no incursion by a unit or grouping of the R.U.C. *as such* . . . In a desperate attempt to prevent imminent murder and having lost surveillance contact in Northern Ireland, it has been established that

two police officers, *unarmed* and in an unmarked car, did drive into Southern Ireland, *but for observation purposes only.*[27] (Emphasis added).

We find this account contradictory and unconvincing. The Chief Constable still appears to assume that his men had some right to pursue their quarry into another country, indicating a disregard for the international law protecting territorial integrity and implying that the security forces do not consider themselves as bound by the rule of law.

The Northern Ireland Standing Advisory Commission on Human Rights and the Use of Firearms by the Security Forces

141. The Northern Ireland Standing Advisory Commission on Human Rights does not have the power to initiate Parliamentary legislation but it makes annual reports to the British Government. In its Ninth Report, published in February 1984, the Commission devoted a chapter and detailed appendix (see Appendix E, below) to the use of firearms by the security forces, recognising that:

> The subject has been one of the most controversial aspects of the security situation in recent years.[28]

We welcome the Commission's recommendation that:

> . . . the wholly different circumstances that pertain in Northern Ireland now, as compared to 1967, require the amendment of the law to embody more clearly the view of Parliament as to the general nature of the circumstances in which potentially lethal force may be used.[29]

The Commission stresses that section 3 (1) of the Criminal Law Act (Northern Ireland) 1967 requires urgent reform:

> . . . the need for legislative change is more pressing in Northern Ireland because of the particular difficulties which confront the police and the armed services here. . .[30]
>
> . . . In principle, we are of the opinion that a police officer or soldier should be entitled to open fire only where it is immediately necessary, or it appears on reasonable grounds to the person using such force to be necessary, either to protect life or to prevent serious injury to himself or to some other person, or where there is a substantial risk that the person to be arrested will cause death or serious injury if his arrest is not effected without delay.[31]

142. We agree broadly with these recommendations and welcome the Commission's work in highlighting the inadequacies of section 3 (1). We emphasise, however, that the European Convention requires 'absolute necessity'. The judicial rulings analysed by the Commission's own working paper at Appendix B of their Ninth Report demonstrate that any weakening of that standard is unacceptable. (See Appendix E, below).

We also believe that the risk that a person may at some future date commit a serious offence should never provide a justification for the use of deadly force. The implication in the last lines of the Commission's paragraph 27 is that Lord Diplock's rationale in the *Attorney-General's Reference* might still be acceptable.

We believe that no room should be left for ambiguity on this question. Only when the person to be arrested presents an immediate threat of death or serious injury may the use of deadly force be permitted, and then only if absolutely necessary in order to prevent death or serious injury.

143. Most witnesses told us that they were sceptical about any effective legal reform as long as the Diplock Courts and the emergency legislation remain in force in Northern Ireland. We are aware of the widespread dissatisfaction these courts and this legislation have engendered among lawyers and significant sections of both Nationalist and Unionist communities. We recommend the repeal of this legislation and the removal of the Diplock Courts below (para. 184 *et seq.*) in the section of our report which deals with the prosecution process.

144. In recommending reform of the 1967 Act in order to ensure compliance with the European Convention, we do not suggest that the political problems of Northern Ireland will be resolved by the simple expedient of reforming the criminal law. Clearly, those problems require political solutions beyond the terms of reference of our Inquiry. We are solely concerned in this section of our Report with the inadequate state of the criminal law, the encouragement given by certain judges to violations of the fundamental human right to life and with the local impact of the many cases we examined.

145. We are satisfied, based on all the evidence we have seen and heard, that the political problems of Northern Ireland have been worsened by violations of Article 2 of the European Convention and Article 6 (1) of the International Covenant on Civil and Political Rights.

The British Government is under a duty at internationl law to act swiftly to remedy these violations. The continued failure to provide adequate remedies for the victims of violations appears to violate Article 13 of the European Convention and would clearly justify the Government of Ireland in bringing an inter-state application under Article 24 of the Convention. This was done in 1971 when internment without trial was re-introduced in the North and the Government of Ireland cited the United Kingdom for torture, inhuman and degrading treatment, contrary to Article 3 of the Convention. (See para. 28 above).

Notes

1. See para. 39, footnote 24 above.
2. See para. 40 above.
3. [1977] A.C. 105, 134.
4. [1975] 3 W.L.R. 11
5. [1975] 3 W.L.R. 11
6. [1977] A.C. 105, 136.
7. [1977] A.C. 105, 136-137.
8. [1977] A.C. 105, 137.
9. [1977] A.C. 105, 132.
10. [1977] A.C. 105, 138. (Emphasis added).
11. N.I.J.B. [1978]
12. [1980] 1 All E.R. 166
13. Greer, D.S. *op. cit.*, pp.151,156.
14. Greer, D.S. *op. cit.*, p.155.
15. *Guardian*, (London) 19 October 1983: 'Self-defence is question, judge tells Waldolf shooting jury'.
   Guardian, 20 October 1983: 'Whose finger on the trigger? – Nick Davies on the increasing use of firearms in the police force'.
16. *Sunday Times*, (London), 8 April 1984: 'Undercover: how Special Branch operates on Belfast's invisible front line'. (Emphasis added).
17. Ibid.
18. *New Statesman*, (London), 15 June 1984, p.10.
19. Ibid.
20. *Irish Times*, Dublin, 6 June 1984.
21. Ibid.
22. *Irish News*, 12 June 1984.
23. *New Statesman*, (London), 11 May 1984.
24. Ibid.
25. *Sunday Press*, 8 April 1984.
26. See McArdle P., *The Secret War*, Mercier Press, 1984. In this book, subtitled 'An account of the sinister activities along the border involving Gardai, RUC, British Army and the SAS', Mr McArdle expands his *Irish Times* article into a detailed catalogue of numerous incursions by British security forces into the Irish Republic.
27. *Irish Times*, Dublin, 9 April 1984.
28. NISACHR, *op. cit.*, para. 21.
29. Ibid. para. 25.
30. Ibid.
31. Ibid. para. 27.

8. Police Investigations of Deaths caused by Members of the Security Forces

146. Our terms of reference require us to review 'the procedures by which the security forces investigate deaths resulting from the use of firearms by their members and the procedures they apply to deaths caused by other persons'.

147. In our chapter on the Diplock Courts and the Prosecuting Authorities (paras. 186 *et seq.*) we describe the provisions of the emergency legislation in Northern Ireland. In this section of our Report we will examine the substantial differences in approach which we found between police investigations of members of the security forces and their investigations of civilians.

148. We have found several investigations by the R.U.C. into deaths caused by members of the security forces to be wholly inadequate. Furthermore, we believe that there is no competent or effective machinery in Northern Ireland for investigating and remedying justifiable complaints against members of the security forces. Members of the security forces are drawn almost exclusively from the Unionist community. This can only lead to a long term loss of confidence by the Nationalist community in the forces of the law. To this extent, the security forces themselves have become part of the political problem of Northern Ireland.

Patterns of Harassment

149. The appearance of heavily armed soldiers in battle fatigues, patrolling the cities, towns and country roads of Northern Ireland has an immediate impact on the visitor. The weaponry carried by the R.U.C. on patrol in their military-looking landrovers shows that the British tradition of unarmed policing does not operate here. To the visitor, the mere sight of the security forces is intimidating.

We are well aware that the security forces face the daily danger of ambush, shooting and bombing and it should be clearly stated that no witness made complaints about the fact that the Army and R.U.C. carry firearms. Complaints were concentrated on abuses of the extensive emergency powers, which responsible community members, lawyers and church leaders perceive to be very widespread.

150. In many of the cases which we examined, a pattern of harassment, threats and intimidation preceded the shooting. We received reports that the interrogation periods of three or seven days permitted under the emergency legislation[1] were employed in the cases of *Seamus Grew* (para. 54), *Neil McMonagle* (para. 59), *Eamonn 'Bronco' Bradley* (para. 60) and *Denis Heaney* (para. 61) to warn either them or their families and friends that the security forces intended to kill them. Further death threats from members of the security forces were reported in the cases of *Tony Harker* and *Ronald Bunting*. (Paras. 49 and 47 respectively).

The power to stop, search and question serves a legitimate purpose when based on reasonable suspicion, but in many cases we heard complaints that these powers were being used to harass or provoke the community. Reasonable suspicion is not required by the emergency legislation and extreme *un*reasonableness characterised the conduct of the security forces on numerous occasions which were brought to our notice.

151. We were particularly disturbed to hear of four incidents in which the security forces had impeded access to emergency medical services:

Neil McMonagle – ambulance stopped by Army until R.U.C. arrived, despite the protests of a local priest, (Para. 59 above);

Danny Barrett – ambulance stopped and crew questioned three times by Army and R.U.C. on the short journey to hospital, (Para. 67);

Patrick Elliott – male nurse, Gerard McGivern, arrested for trying to give first aid, then ambulance turned away when the nurse said he believed Elliott was dead but that he was not medically qualified to certify death, (Para. 68);

Martin Malone – Brian McArdle was assaulted by a soldier striking him in the mouth as he went to telephone for a doctor, (Para. 50).

In the Martin Malone case the police did not visit the scene for several hours after his death and the U.D.R. patrol which shot him apparently left Malone lying dead at the scene without taking any further action (see Cardinal Ó Fiaich's statement at Malone's funeral, para. 50).

152. In at least three cases which we examined, the security forces used their extensive powers to search private homes without warrants a short time after the killings, when they visited or raided the homes of the deceased and failed to inform their families of the death: Liam Prince, (para. 51); Gervaise McKerr, (para. 55); and Patrick Elliott, (para. 67). In the further instance of Danny Barrett, (para. 67), shot as he sat on his family's front garden wall, the Army responded by searching the home in an oppressive fashion. We can only conclude that the purpose of these searches was to try to find some evidence *ex post facto* to justify the killing. Even accepting that as the motive, the cold inhumanity of refusing to inform families of these deaths is particularly disturbing.

Differential Treatment

153. Practising and academic lawyers in Northern Ireland alleged that the R.U.C. routinely deny access to legal advice to suspects interrogated under the emergency legislation. The earliest time at which solicitors are allowed to see their clients is normally after a period of 48 hours detention. We regard this practice as oppressive and unjustified.

By contrast, in cases where members of the security forces have been interrogated by the R.U.C. they have received almost immediate access to legal advice: Privates Jones and Bailey in the *Bradley* case, (para. 60) and 'Soldier A' in the *Barrett case,* (para. 67). Even more disturbing is the extract from Hutton J.'s judgment in *Lynch* v. *Ministry of Defence* (1983) 6 N.I.J.B. where the regimental message log read:

> *Soldiers involved in incident not to be interviewed by R.U.C. – R.U.C. want to interview them, stall them – telephone me and I will dispatch the Flying Lawyer.* (Emphasis added) (See para. 66).

The *Prince* case (para. 51) also suggests that the Army has obstructed the investigation of its members by the R.U.C., since we were informed that an R.U.C. sergeant told the family that his 'hands were tied' and that they would 'never get to the truth of the matter because of the controversial circumstances surrounding the shooting'.

Complaints Procedures

154. For a number of years, the absence of democratic account-ability by the police has been a source of public anxiety in Britain, Ireland and the United States. In Northern Ireland, however, despite the stringent criticisms in the Hunt Report,[2] the R.U.C. appears to have no effective complaints procedure. In November 1981 the Government announced a review of the procedure but in the Report of the Standing Advisory Commission on Human Rights, published in February 1984 there is only one paragraph headed 'Police Com-plaints'. It reads:

> In our last Annual Report we said that we would be examining the Government's proposals for changes to the police complaints pro-cedures in Northern Ireland. These have not yet been published. Although these proposals may be expected to follow closely those now being developed for the police complaints procedure in England and Wales, we hope that the different circumstances in Northern Ireland will be fully recognised, especially in the conciliation process and that the proposals ultimately adopted will be such as to command the con-fidence both of the police and of the general public.[3]

The complaints procedures proposed for England and Wales under the Police and Criminal Evidence Bill 1983,[4] have themselves been questioned by many commentators and we regret that the Advisory Committee has not offered more specific advice on how to ensure full recognition for the 'different circumstances in Northern Ireland'. We believe that the creation of a democratically accountable police complaints procedure is a vital element in the effort which must be made to increase public confidence in the security forces.

155. The National Council for Civil Liberties, in their evidence to Sir George Baker, described complaints procedures in Northern Ire-land as 'totally inadequate'. Baker found that:

> There was a feeling that when abuses had occurred action had rarely been taken to punish the offender; and that even if steps were taken the results were never seen by the complainant and the public.[5]

And further:

> The belief is widespread that it is no use complaining because nothing will happen. Even if unjustified, this belief inhibits co-operation with and support for the RUC.[6]

However, having noted that only 2.75% of complaints received by the R.U.C. in 1982 were found justified,[7] and that the Police and Criminal Evidence Bill proposes to set up a Police Complaints Authority, Baker concludes this part of his review with the words:

> In this fluid situation I do not consider that any specific recommendation by me is desirable save that consideration be given to the dissatisfaction, disquiet and concern that I have endeavoured to highlight and especially the need to give the complainant full and speedy information. The R.U.C. have an extremely difficult job to do in which they need the utmost co-operation from everybody.[8]

156. We received a number of specific complaints. We were told that Seamus Grew made a formal report of an attempt on his life only to find himself arrested and held for three days' interrogation. He then filed a formal complaint that R.U.C. officers had threatened he would be 'in his box before Christmas'. He was killed by the R.U.C.'s undercover surveillance unit before that Christmas. Subsequently, a member of the Ulster Defence Regiment was charged with having attempted to murder Grew in the incident which Grew had reported to the R.U.C. (See para. 54).

We were also informed that Ronald Bunting complained that R.U.C. officers threatened him with death. His formal complaint resulted in a criminal charge of 'wasting police time' on which he was convicted. Shortly after winning his appeal he too was shot dead, allegedly by Unionist paramilitaries. (See para. 47).

Father Murray, Father Faul, Ms Bernadette Devlin McAliskey and others told us that police complaints procedures are widely regarded as a waste of time. Many lawyers said they believe that the R.U.C. are unable to investigate the Army and that they lack the will to investigate their own officers.

Public Accountability and the Security Forces

157. An embattled, militarised police force under constant threat of armed attack inevitably views outside (or, for that matter, internal) investigations as attempts to undermine its morale. There are certain Unionist politicians who routinely urge the Government to let the security forces 'take their gloves off'. After a decade and a half of continuing loss of life and property in Northern Ireland we cannot be surprised that such policies are advocated.

But if, disregarding law and morality, the police and army were allowed to operate without restraint, effecively to intern suspects without trial, to brutalise them in the attempt to obtain information and, when all else fails, to execute summarily those whom they believe responsible for acts of political violence, the question still remains: will this solve the political problem or merely make it worse?

In Northern Ireland since 1969 the security forces, using wide emergency powers, have detained suspects without trial and brutalised them in interrogations.[9] Several witnesses told us that they believe summary executions have occurred in some cases.

If nothing else remains clear after 15 years of bloodshed, it is certain that the political problem has not found a political solution. We believe that the powers given to the security forces are a part of the problem. Unless such powers are exercised under a system of democratic accountability, hostility towards the security forces is bound to grow.

Towards an Independent Review Procedure

158. We believe that there is an urgent need for impartial machinery to investigate and determine complaints against the security forces. A board or commission should be established on which all communities in Northern Ireland and the security forces themselves would be represented.

This body should also have the duty to review policy matters, including the use of force. It should have the power to adjudicate on police misconduct, with power to subpoena witnesses and to issue findings and recommendations for immediate specific action. Where the security forces oppose any recommendations, a final adjudicating body should have the power to enforce decisions in appropriate cases.

159. An effective review body would foster greater respect for the law. At present in Northern Ireland a significant section of the public believes that the security forces can operate outside the law. Some members of the security forces may themselves share this belief. The more such a belief is held, the greater the need for determined action to stamp it out.

Community Representation in the Security Forces

160. At the time of the Hunt Report[10] the proportion of Catholics

in the R.U.C. was put at 11%, with no Catholics at all in the paramilitary 'Specials'. According to *The Belfast Bulletin*, a decade after Hunt, Catholics constituted only 4% of the R.U.C. and 2% of the U.D.R.[11]

It is clear that alienation is inevitable where Catholics amount to approximately 40% of the population of Northern Ireland and only provide an infinitesimal proportion of the province's security forces.

Many police forces in the United States, faced with a similar imbalance in Black, Hispanic and other minority recruitment, have instituted 'affirmative action' hiring programmes and policies in recent years. The experience of the United States members of the Inquiry is that these programmes, while not panaceas for discrimination, have contributed towards the easing of tensions in divided communities.

Moreover, in Northern Ireland the only alternative is to do nothing and allow Catholic representation in the security forces to diminish still further. If public confidence in the R.U.C. is the goal of the Government then we believe that positive steps must be taken to increase the proportion of Catholics in the security forces.

Notes

1. The Northern Ireland (Emergency Provisions) Act, 1978 provides for 72 hours detention (Section 11). The Prevention of Terrorism Act (1984) permits detention for a total period of 7 days but authorisation must be obtained from the Secretary of State to detain for longer than 48 hours (Section 12). (See below, para. 195).

2. *Report of the Advisory Committee on Police in Northern Ireland*, (Hunt Report), Cmnd. 535, HMSO, Belfast, October 1969. See above, para. 30.

3. *Ninth Report of the Standing Advisory Commission on Human Rights*, (NISACHR Report), HC 262, 1984, para. 29.

4. The Police and Criminal Evidence Bill had been under debate in the Westminster Parliament for many months after the conclusion of work on our report. For a detailed critique of its many inroads into civil liberties see Christian L., *Policing by Coercion*, 1983, published by the Greater London Council Police Committee Support Unit.

5. *Review of the Operation of the Northern Ireland (Emergency Provisions) Act 1978*, (Baker Report), Cmnd. 9222, HMSO London, April 1984, para. 324

6. Ibid., para. 325

7. Ibid., para. 332

8. Ibid., para. 338

9. *Report of the Committee of Inquiry into Police Interrogation Procedures in Northern Ireland*, (Bennett Report), Cmnd. 7497, HMSO March 1979. *Amnesty International Mission to Northern Ireland*, Report, May 1978. Taylor P., *Beating the Terrorists?*, 1980, Penguin.

10. *Report of the Advisory Committee on Police in Northern Ireland*, (Hunt Report), Cmnd. 535, HMSO, Belfast, October 1969. See above, para. 30.

11. *Belfast Bulletin No.10*, 1980.

9. Coroners' Inquests

161. Our terms of reference include: 'the role of the Coroners' Courts in the investigations of deaths resulting from the use of firearms by the security forces'. We therefore sought to establish the extent to which Northern Ireland Coroners' Courts are equipped to carry out fully independent and impartial inquiries into causes of death where civilians are killed by members of the security forces in disputed circumstances.

162. We received detailed written submissions on this subject from civil liberties organisations, including: the Committee on the Administration of Justice (Northern Ireland); Inquest: United Campaigns for Justice (Britain); National Council for Civil Liberties (Britain); Northern Ireland Association of Socialist Lawyers; Northern Ireland Civil Rights Association. We also heard oral evidence from Dr Tom Hadden, Queen's University, Belfast and from solicitors Gus Campbell, Paschal O'Hare and Joseph Rice.

163. We are convinced, on the basis of the cases examined and the testimony received, that where civilians are shot dead by members of the security forces on duty, the Northern Ireland Coroners' Courts lack the capacity to carry out fully independent and impartial inquiries into the causes of death. They are also unable to ensure that proper action is taken by the authorities to prevent the avoidable recurrence of such killings.

We find that Inquests are delayed unreasonably, sometimes for explicitly political reasons; material witnesses are not summoned to attend and give evidence and unreliable scientific evidence has been accepted. Finally, we note that the law regulating Coroners' Courts in Northern Ireland has been changed to deprive juries of the power to return verdicts and to make recommendations for preventing similar deaths in the future.

Historical Role of Coroners' Courts

164. These courts were established to inquire into unexpected, unexplained or suspicious deaths; to ascertain the facts and to assure the public that any necessary action would be taken promptly by the authorities to prevent similar fatalities in future. As early as the 13th century the Coroner was required to go immediately to the place where a sudden death had occurred, to bring before him the representatives of the four nearest townships, and to inquire *where* the person was slain, *who* was there, and *who* was guilty. [1]

165. More recently, however, the Coroners' powers have become much more circumscribed in Northern Ireland, as well as in England and Wales. Under the Special Powers Acts, in force between 1922 and 1972, Section 10 gave the Northern Ireland Minister of Home Affairs power to prohibit the holding of inquests by coroners on dead bodies in any area in the North. This ban could be total or limited to a particular inquest, 'for the purpose of preserving the peace and maintaining order'.[2] This power never extended to England and Wales.

The Duty to Hold an Inquest

166. A Coroner may hold an Inquest without a jury except where there is reason to suspect that:

> The death occurred in prison; or. . .
> The death occurred in circumstances the continuance or possible recurrence of which is prejudicial to the health or safety of the public or any section of the public.[3]

We were told that, despite these express provisions, in the Inquest on the death of *Julie Livingstone,* a 14 year old West Belfast girl killed by a plastic bullet in May 1981, the Coroner refused to empanel a jury, although plastic bullets posed a constant threat to life and health. (See above, para. 70 *et seq.*) The High Court ruled that the Inquest should be held with a jury and the Belfast Coroner withdrew from the case. The jury found that Miss Livingstone was the 'totally innocent victim' of a plastic bullet.

167. We agree with all expert witnesses in concluding that in every case where a member of the security forces is suspected of having killed a civilian the law must require that the Coroner should sit with a jury.

168. We view the present system for summoning juries in Northern Ireland as undesirable. Under Section 18(1) of the Coroners Act (Northern Ireland) 1959, the jury is to be summoned by the police. Where the death may have been caused by the security forces and especially where, as has most often been the case, the deceased was from the Nationalist community which is disturbingly under-represented in the ranks of the security forces, then the police should play no role in summoning the jury.

We therefore believe that the Coroners' Juries Act 1983, operative in England and Wales, should be extended to Northern Ireland so that the Coroner's Officer would receive a list of jurors selected at random and be instructed to summon those listed in strict order.

The Duty to Hold an Inquest Promptly

169. In Northern Ireland, as in England and Wales, the Coroner must hold an inquest: 'as soon as practicable after the Coroner has been notified of the death'.[4]

However, if the police inform the Coroner that a person may be charged with murder, manslaughter or certain other prescribed offences, the Coroner is then required to adjourn the inquest for 28 days.[5] At any time before the adjourned date the police may request a further adjournment. The Coroner has a discretion whether or not to grant further adjournments.[6]

In England and Wales, Coroners will normally open an inquest formally and then adjourn it for the police and Director of Public Prosecutions to complete their investigations. The public is given the reasons for any adjournment.

170. However, in Northern Ireland, the practice of Coroners seems to be to postpone the opening of inquests until the police and D.P.P. announce that they are ready to proceed. In many cases which we examined, this practice has led to unwarranted delays in opening inquests. In particular, we note the public statement of the Coroner for Armagh on 3 September 1983 that:

> I have a public duty to hold every Inquest as soon as practicable and this duty has been largely negated by the unexplained delay by the D.P.P. Such unexplained delay has caused the agony of suspense and a sense of frustration to all concerned which is contrary to the principles of natural and constitutional justice.[7]

The Coroner was referring to the killings of McKerr, Toman and Burns by the R.U.C. near Lurgan or 11 November 1982 (See para.55 above); Michael Tighe, also near Lurgan on 24 November 1982; and of Grew and Carroll on 12 December in Armagh (see para.54 above). Tony Harker's inquest (see para.49 above) was adjourned eight times between March 1982 and May 1983. According to Father Denis Faul, the inquest on Jack McCartan, shot dead in 1977 while leaving the Andersonstown Social Club was adjourned for a total of 18 months. The inquest into the killing of 15 year-old Danny Barrett, (see para. 67 above) was delayed 13 months although the D.P.P. decided not to prosecute.

The Armagh Coroner has now resigned over 'grave irregularities' in the R.U.C. files on the Grew/Carroll case, his successor will not preside over the inquest due to his 'professional commitments' and an investigation by Greater Manchester police officers into the R.U.C.'s handling of the case has meant a further adjournment, (see para. 54 above). Over two years have passed since the killings and no inquest has been held on any of the Armagh cases which first aroused the concern of Amnesty International in 1982, (see para. 7 above).

171. When these criticisms of unwarranted delay were referred to the Lord Chancellor, the senior judicial figure in the United Kingdom, he replied:

> Given the unprecedented volume of crimes of violence in Northern Ireland, the consequent strain on police and forensic resources, and the need to allow the Director of Public Prosecutions sufficient time in which to investigate the frequently confused circumstances of a particular violent death, there are (I would suggest) *legitimate administrative and policy reasons for the delay* associated with some inquests in the Province.[8]

172. The maxim 'justice delayed is justice denied' holds especially true of Coroners' Inquests in the special circumstances we investigated in Northern Ireland. Such deliberate delays normally end in a decision not to prosecute, leaving relatives and local communities with the sense of injustice described by the Armagh Coroner. Indeed, we were told that less than 8% of those killings of unarmed civilians by members of the security forces in disputed circumstances have resulted in criminal charges against members of the security forces.

173. We heard that both the Unionist and Nationalist communities

in Northern Ireland see the Inquest as the only place to find out the truth behind a killing. Relatives may sometimes need adjournments in order to obtain counsel or to conduct scientific tests. However, where delays are requested by the security forces themselves or the D.P.P. for 'policy reasons', the only conclusion that can be drawn is that a 'cooling-off' period is being sought in the hope that local concern will subside.

We are disturbed by the Lord Chancellor's opinion that reasons of policy might justify delay. This seems to justify political interference in the administration of justice. In our view, no other policy interest can take precedence over the public interest in inquests being held, as required by statute, 'as soon as reasonably practicable'.

In the case of the shooting of Steven Waldorf, no 'legitimate policy reasons' were seen for delaying the D.P.P.'s decision to prosecute two London police officers (see observations of Cardinal Ó Fiaich at para. 50 above) and, indeed, that decision was reached with exemplary speed.

Material Witnesses

174. We heard evidence in case after case where the member of the security forces who fired the fatal shot was not called to testify. Instead, his statement was read out and, in some cases, other members of the security forces gave oral testimony.

This practice seems to have grown out of Rule 9(2) of the 1980 Amendment to the Northern Ireland Coroners Rules which provides that persons suspected of causing the death or charged with or likely to be charged with the death shall not be compelled to give evidence.

This provision has no counterpart in England and Wales where the privilege against self-incrimination is a sufficient shield for a witness who may be charged with the death. We believe it is fundamentally unjust to excuse any member of the security forces from attending to testify, especially where the result is that untested written statements are accepted and parties are denied the opportunity to cross-examine witnesses on what may be highly controversial assertions. (See, for example, the *McMonagle* case. para. 59 above).

Indeed, in the Danny Barrett inquest (see above, para. 67), we heard that the jury expressly rejected the statement of 'Soldier A', who did not appear, in which he claimed that the person he shot had been carrying a rifle. The jury, however, found that the deceased was sitting on a wall and 'the deceased was not a gunman or a rioter'.

Further cases in which we were told that such anonymous 'Soldier A' statements were offered and/or admitted in evidence included the inquests on Liam Prince (para. 51), Gary English (para. 179 below), Patrick Elliott (para. 68), Paddy Duffy (para. 62) and Denis Heaney (para. 61). In some cases it appeared that only when families went to the expense of retaining Queen's Counsel were Coroners prepared to insist on live evidence from the security forces.

175. We believe that the rule in England and Wales should apply also in Northern Ireland, namely that written statements should not be admissible unless they are unlikely to be disputed or else if the maker of the statement is unable to give oral evidence within a reasonable period.[9]

176. An amendment to the Coroners Rules recently abolished the duty of the Northern Ireland Coroners to 'examine on oath . . : *all persons who tender their evidence* respecting the facts and all persons whom he thinks it expedient to examine as being likely to have knowledge of the relevant facts' (our emphasis). [10] While this is still the law for England and Wales, the rules in Northern Ireland now give the Coroner complete discretion whether to hear any witness who comes forward or whether to summon one who does not.

The danger of abuse arising from this wide discretion was demonstrated in the inquest into the killing of Stephen McConomy, shot in the back of the head by a plastic bullet at close range in April 1981. At the inquest 14 months later, the family's lawyer was unable to cross-examine the soldier who killed the 11 year old boy because the Coroner admitted a 'Soldier A' statement into evidence. When the lawyer tried to question other soldiers present in the same armoured carrier with the Lance Corporal who had fired the plastic bullet the Coroner tried to prevent his questions about riot gun training on the grounds that those soldiers were not the ones who had fired the shot.[11]

177. We believe that the Coroner should be compelled to hear all witnesses who present themselves so long as their evidence is relevant. Given the practical difficulties of relying on the security forces to conduct all necessary inquiries into killings caused by members of the security forces, any 'properly interested person' (see below) should be entitled to call witnesses to material facts.

178. The 1963 Coroners Rules for Northern Ireland provide that:

any person who in the opinion of the coroner is a properly interested person shall be entitled to examine any witness at an inquest either in person or by counsel or solicitor.[12]

However, the definition of 'interested persons' applicable in England and Wales[13] does not extend to Northern Ireland. It specifies classes of persons (e.g. 'the parent, child, spouse or any personal representative of the deceased'). Persons who have been held 'properly interested' in England and Wales have included local authorities for the area in which the death occurred and, in the case of Blair Peach, a school teacher killed by the police during an anti-fascist demonstration in London, the Anti-Nazi League, of which he was a member was declared 'properly interested'.

179. The ability of 'properly interested persons' to present evidence or examine witnesses will often be limited by financial circumstances. In the case of *Gary English,* who, together with James Brown, was run over by a British Army landrover on the streets of Derry, his father, Michael English testified that he has spent over £7,000 to obtain expert scientific evidence which proved forensically that the government scientist's evidence was mostly inaccurate. Part of the cost was incurred because no independent forensic science laboratory exists in any part of Ireland and an expert had to be brought from Denmark (see para. 46 above). Additionally, Mr English had to pay for a Queen's Counsel to represent him and ensure that the soldiers did not merely submit written statements.

180. All of our witnesses stressed the need for free legal aid (state-paid legal fees) for properly interested persons. We fully agree that the burden imposed on Mr English is one which no family should be forced to bear in such circumstances and we therefore recommend that Legal Aid be available both for legal representation and for the preparation and presentation of relevant forensic scientific and autopsy evidence.

As long ago as 1980 the British House of Commons Select Committee on Home Affairs recommended legal aid for interested parties in inquests. Ten years ago the Legal Aid Act 1974 made provision for this to be done, but the relevant schedule has never been brought into operation.[14]

181. The ability to cross-examine and to represent an interested party properly is dependent on the legal representative being given access to relevant documentary material, and especially to police

reports on the death. We endorse the view that such access should be made compulsory.

The Role of the Coroners' Juries

182. There is a major difference between the rules in Northern Ireland and in England and Wales in the power of the jury to bring in verdicts. Indeed, in Northern Ireland, since the 1980 amendments to the rules, juries are allowed only to make 'findings', as distinct from verdicts. Before those rules came into effect, a jury in Northern Ireland was not allowed to bring in a verdict of 'unlawful killing' by an unnamed person, a verdict which is available to a jury in England and Wales. Thus, if the jury was dissatisfied with the explanation given by the security forces, or even if they believed the security forces to be guilty of murder, the only verdict available was an 'open verdict'.

In England and Wales 'no verdict shall be framed in such a way as to appear to determine any question of (a) criminal liability on the part of a named person, or (b) civil liability'.[15] This contrasts sharply with the Northern Ireland rule that:

> neither the coroner nor the jury shall express any opinion on questions of criminal or civil liability.[16]

The only findings they may make are: 'who the deceased was, how, when and where he came by his death.'[17] This means, in practice, that an English or Welsh jury could bring in a verdict of 'unlawful killing' where a member of the security forces had used more force than absolutely necessary, though it could not name an individual. In Northern Ireland, if a jury reaches that conclusion, it could previously do no more than record an 'open verdict'. Today it may not even do that but is limited to listing its actual findings.

183. We feel bound to conclude that the recent amendments to the Coroners' rules in Northern Ireland have been designed to protect members of the security forces from all public criticism, justified or otherwise. This is confirmed again by the Lord Chancellor, this time in his 14 March 1983 letter to Lord Hylton:

> A 'killing unlawfully' finding would I believe be a potent source of difficulty in Northern Ireland and I consider that it would be a retrograde step to turn coroners' enquiries into trials going beyond the finding of facts by re-introducing the attribution of blame.[18]

We believe it is most important that juries should be free to reach a verdict of 'unlawful killing' by an unnamed person. This is especially important in Northern Ireland, where the authorities have demonstrated an unwillingness to bring members of the security forces before the courts. The Coroner's inquest provides a safety valve for public concern and an open public forum in which the security forces and all other interested parties can ensure that matters of important public interest are not swept under the carpet.

Notes

1. 4 Edward 1, Statute 2, 1275: *De Officio Coronatoris*.
2. Civil Authorities (Special Powers) Act 1922, Section 10 (1).
3. Coroners' Act (Northern Ireland) 1959, s.18.
4. Coroners' (Practice and Procedure) Rules, 1963 ('the 1963 Rules'), Rule 3; as amended by Coroners' (Practice and Procedure) (Amendment) Rules, 1980 ('the 1980 Rules').
5. 1963 Rules, Rule 12 (1), as amended by the 1980 Rules, Rule 12.
6. 1963 Rules, Rule 12 (2).
7. Evidence to Inquiry of Joseph Rice, Solicitor.
8. Letter to Lord Hylton, 7 June 1983.
9. Coroners' Rules (England and Wales) 1953, Rule 28; as substituted by 1980 Rules (S.I.1980 No. 557).
10. 1980 Rules amendment to 1963 Rules, Rule 8 (1).
11. Lord T. Gifford Q.C., *Death on the Streets of Derry*, N.C.C.L., London 1983.
12. 1963 Rules, Rule 7 (1).
13. Coroners' (Practice and Procedure)(Amendment) Rules 1980, (S.R.O. No.444)
14. House of Commons Select Committee on Home Affairs, 1980 HC 613. Legal Aid Act 1974 (Schedule 7).
15. Coroners' Rules (England and Wales) 1953, Rule 33; as substituted by Coroners' (Amendment) Rules 1977.
16. 1963 Rules, Rule 33.
17. 1963 Rules, Rule 16
18. Letter to Lord Hylton, 14 March 1983.

10. The Diplock Courts and the Prosecuting Authorities

184. We are satisfied, from the evidence of numerous witnesses, that the non-jury 'Diplock' Courts are central to the amount of public dissatisfaction with the administration of justice. Everyone charged under the emergency legislation in Northern Ireland is tried by a single judge, sitting without a jury. We give a brief outline of the history and functions of the courts here, but for a more detailed analysis readers should see the publications listed in the bibliography at Appendix C.

History of the Diplock Courts

185. In the worsening political and security climate following the re-introduction of internment without trial in August 1971 and the Bloody Sunday killings of January 1972 (see above, paras. 27 and 28) the British authorities decided to prorogue the Northern Ireland Parliament. Direct rule from Westminster was instituted in March 1972 and the Government undertook to review the Special Powers Act (see paras.11 to 14 above).

186. Lord Diplock, a senior judge of the House of Lords (see paras. 108 to 112 above) was asked by the British Government to report on:

> What arrangements for the administration of justice in Northern Ireland could be made in order to deal more effectively with terrorist organisations by bringing to book, otherwise than by internment by the Executive, individuals involved in terrorist activities, particularly those who plan and direct, but do not necessarily take part in, terrorist acts.[1]

187. Lord Diplock's report was completed within two months and its recommendations were enacted in 1973 in the form of the Northern Ireland (Emergency Provisions) Act. The Act currently in force is the Northern Ireland (Emergency Provisions) Act 1978 (EPA78) and all references will be to section numbers in that Act. The EPA, as its full title implies, extends only to Northern Ireland. Since 1974, emergency legislation applicable to both Northern Ireland and Britain has been in force in the form of the Prevention of Terrorism Act (PTA) which will be considered below.

188. The Emergency Provisions Act implemented Lord Diplock's recommendations by abolishing the right to jury trial for all offences connected with 'terrorism'. The Act defined terrorism as:

> The use of violence for political ends and includes any use of violence for the purpose of putting the public or any section of the public in fear.[2]

The Act further removes the presumption that a person charged with an offence is entitled to bail. Instead it places the burden on the accused of satisfying a senior judge that the accused will comply with stringent bail conditions.[3]

189. At British common law the prosecution must prove beyond reasonable doubt that an accused person's alleged confession was not obtained by threats, inducements or oppressive conduct. Lord Diplock, however, recommended that statements should be admitted into evidence even when obtained:

> . . . as a result of building up a psychological atmosphere in which the initial desire of the person being questioned to remain silent is replaced by an urge to confide in the questioner, or statements preceded by promises of favours or indications of the consequences which might follow if the person questioned persisted in refusing to answer.[4]

190. The EPA further provides that where such a confession is produced by the prosecution, the burden of proof shifts to the defendant to prove a *prima facie* case of:

> torture, inhuman or degrading treatment in order to induce him to make the statement.[5]

If the defendant is able to meet that burden, then the prosecution must prove its case beyond a reasonable doubt.

191. The accused also has the burden of proof where a weapon is found at premises where she/he is a habitual visitor. In that event the defendant must show *prima facie* that:

> he did not at that time know of its presence in the premises in question or, if he did know, that he had no control over it.[6]

192. Under the Act, the Secretary of State for Northern Ireland has absolute authority to proscribe organisations and membership in such organisations is punishable with up to 10 years' imprisonment.[7] Detention without trial (internment) has been suspended since December 1975, but the power to re-introduce it remains.[8]

193. Common law police powers are replaced by special powers under which the security forces do not require a search warrant to search homes or other buildings in connection with 'terrorist offences'.[9] Mere 'suspicion' replaces the common law necessity for 'reasonable suspicion' in entitling a member of the security forces to make an arrest.[10]

194. Neither 'reasonableness' nor 'suspicion' are required for the right to stop and search any member of the public and if that person fails to answer to the best of his or her ability all questions concerning identity and recent movements such failure is punishable with up to six months' imprisonment.[11]

195. The ability of the R.U.C. to obtain confessions·is greatly enhanced by Section 11 of the EPA and Section 12 of the PTA, which permit the police to detain a person for interrogation for up to 72 hours (EPA) or, after an initial 48 hours, for a further 5 days (PTA). Suspects are not permitted access to legal advice until at least 48 hours have elapsed. It is noteworthy that, according to the R.U.C., of those arrested under these powers in Northern Ireland, *some 76% are released without charge.*[12] The figures for Britain are even more startling with 95% of persons arrested under the PTA section 12 released without charge.[13]

196. The Prevention of Terrorism Act 1984 replaces the Act of 1976. Unlike the EPA, the PTA applies to the whole of the U.K., although a person charged under the PTA in Northern Ireland will be tried by a Diplock Court judge, while a person charged identically in Britain will receive a jury trial.

197. The Labour Government which first introduced the legislation in 1974, following the Birmingham pub bombing outrages, described it as 'draconian'. Under the PTA a citizen of the U.K. may be 'excluded' (deported) from Britain to Northern Ireland (or *vice versa*). The Act empowers the Secretary of State to exclude a person if he is satisfied that such person has been concerned in or may attempt to be concerned in 'the commission, preparation or instigation of acts of terrorism'.[14]

198. As noted above (para. 195), the PTA enables the police to detain a person for questioning for an initial period of 48 hours, after which, with the Secretary of State's approval, detention and interrogation may continue for a further 5 days. The Secretary of State has almost invariably approved these extended periods.[15]

199. The PTA contains a specific offence of 'withholding information', under which any person who fails to disclose to the security forces 'as soon as reasonably practicable' information which:

> he knows or believes might be of material assistance
>
> > (a) in preventing the commission by any other person of an act of terrorism. . . , or
> >
> > (b) in securing the apprehension, prosecution or conviction of any person for an offence involving the commission, preparation or instigation of an act of terrorism. . .'[16]

is guilty of an offence punishable with up to 5 years imprisonment.

The Impact of the Diplock Courts

200. We received a considerable amount of evidence from academic and practising lawyers and from civil rights organisations and community representatives that the emergency legislation and the Diplock Courts have alienated a substantial part of the population of Northern Ireland from the administration of justice. The Inquiry heard that this reaction is not confined to the Nationalist community but is also felt in significant sections of the Unionist population.

201. The extensive powers available to the security forces have led to many well-substantiated allegations of abuse during the past 10 years. In 1971 the Government of Ireland took the United Kingdom Government before the European Commission of Human Rights and ultimately obtained a judgment from the European Court condemning as 'inhuman and degrading' the treatment of those detained without trial (see para. 29 above). Amnesty International and the British Government's Bennett Report attested to brutality in interrogations before 1978. Lord Gifford's recent report on the 'Supergrass' system of paid informers has documented more recent abuses.[17]

202. During the course of our Inquiry into the circumstances of several killings of unarmed civilians, witnesses made constant reference to abuses of the security forces' powers under these emergency statutes. Particularly frequent were allegations of abuses in searches of homes, detention and interrogation of persons who were not suspects, repeated stopping, searching and questioning of the same person by the same members of the security forces and other abuses constituting patterns of harassment and intimidation.

203. Complaining about such abuses is widely regarded as futile (see paras. 154 to 156 above) and several witnesses told us that they have reluctantly come to accept that harassment forms a part of their daily lives. We believe that the powers available to the security forces are too broad and unrestrained.

204. Both the EPA and the PTA have been reviewed recently by Government-appointed Inquiries but none have been invited to consider whether the legislation should continue on the statute books. As Britain's National Council of Civil Liberties observed in its paper on the new PTA:

> Experience in Northern Ireland, which has had emergency powers since 1922, shows that such powers are not a necessary, acceptable and effective response to political violence but one of the chief causes of continued violence. The denial of civil rights feeds the conflict from which the paramilitary emerges. It breeds greater contempt for the Government and for the legal system.[18]

All of the evidence presented to our Inquiry supports this view and we accept the opinion of the National Council for Civil Liberties that the ordinary criminal law is adequate to deal with violence in Northern Ireland and the rest of the United Kingdom.

The Diplock Judges

205. Almost ten years ago, Boyle, Hadden and Hillyard noted:

> the feeling in Republican circles that the courts and the judiciary were part and parcel of the Unionist power structure. . .[19]

They recorded that:

> At the height of the civil rights campaign in the late 1960s two of the three judges in the Northern Ireland Court of Appeal were ex-Attorneys-General in Unionist governments; one of the four High Court judges was likewise an ex-Attorney-General, and another the son of an Attorney-General; two of the County Court judges were ex-Unionist MPs and another the son of a Unionist MP. . .

206. It is not unusual in Britain, the Irish Republic or the United States for judicial appointments to be made from members of political parties. What is exceptional about Northern Ireland is the sectarian history of the one political party from which these appoint-

ments were made. The Westminster Government always sought to ensure that at least one senior judge was a Catholic but the Nationalist community could not be expected to regard this as more than 'tokenism'.

207. In our review of judicial decisions on the legality of the use of firearms by the security forces, we were struck by the number of occasions on which the same judges' names recurred, either sitting as single judge at first instance in the Diplock Court or as one of the three judge bench in the Court of Appeals. The Haldane Society noted in its 1980 publication, 'Diplock and the Assault on Civil Liberties':

> The very size of the judiciary means that the same judges take turns at hearing cases at first instance and then sitting on appeals. Although they do not, of course, hear appeals from their own decisions, this process of 'taking in each other's dirty laundry' cannot avoid giving a public impression of the old boy network at work.[20]

208. As we have already noted (see above, paras. 130 and 134 to 135) Lord Justice Gibson and Mr Justice MacDermott have both contributed substantially to the perception in the Nationalist community and elsewhere that the principal function of the Diplock Courts is to uphold the actions of the security forces. When police officers are congratulated on their marksmanship in killing unarmed men and such killings are described as bringing unconvicted people to 'the final court of justice', public distrust of the courts is increased. The view of the judges fuelled the belief that similar attitudes have lain behind the acquittals of soldiers previously charged with murder or manslaughter.

209. We accept that some acquittals of members of the security forces may result as much from inadequate investigations, deliberate concealment of evidence or half-hearted prosecuting as from judicial bias. However, where no jury sits to represent the community, it is the judge who must be seen as bearing the ultimate responsibility for the verdict.

The Attorney-General and the Director of Public Prosecutions

210. Until 1972 Northern Ireland had its own Attorney-General. With the abolition of the Northern Ireland Parliament this function passed to the Attorney-General in Westminster. He plays a central role in all cases where any question of prosecuting a member of the

security forces arises and, as a member of the British Government,
he is able to exercise political influence over such prosecutions.

211. Dr Tom Hadden, of the Law Faculty, The Queen's University,
Belfast, provided us with the submissions prepared by himself and
Professor Kevin Boyle, Steven Greer and Dermot Walsh to Sir George
Baker's review of the EPA in 1983. Although it is officially asserted
that members of the security forces are subject to the rule of law in
the same way as anyone else, Dr Hadden and his colleagues point
out that:

> The legal reality is somewhat different. In the first place investigations
> by the police and Army in such cases are often alleged to be perfunctory.
> Members of the security forces are certainly not subject to the same
> interrogation procedures as others and there is bound to be a suspicion
> of a lack of impartiality and persistence in these investigations. In the
> second place the Director of Public Prosecutions is *not* wholly indepen-
> dent. Under the Prosecution of Offences Order (Northern Ireland) 1972
> it is clear that the Director is formally subject to the Attorney-General,
> and it has been publicly admitted that difficult cases, like those involving
> members of the security forces, are regularly discussed by the Director
> and the Attorney-General. (Emphasis in the original).

The public admission referred to was made in a speech by the current
Attorney-General, Sir Michael Havers, at Queen's University,
Belfast, on 16 October 1979.

212. A senior practising lawyer told us that the Attorney-General's
representative spends two to three days a week in Northern Ireland
overseeing the work of the Director of Public Prosecutions.

213. The importance of his role can be gauged from the fact that
the Attorney-General himself elected to prosecute the two police
officers charged with the attempted murder of Mr Steven Waldorf
in London. (See para. 123 above). The fact that no Attorney-General
has ever conducted the prosecution of any member of the security
forces in Northern Ireland was repeatedly mentioned by witnesses
at our hearings. We believe that the impression in the communities
we visited is that there is one law for the British and one law for
those who live in Northern Ireland.

214. However, Ed Moloney of the *Irish Times* has reported that
senior British Government sources confirmed that Sir Michael
Havers originally intended to lead the prosecution team in the trials
of the three R.U.C. officers charged with the murder of Eugene
Toman. (See para. 55 above). According to Mr Moloney, the Attorney-

General was dissuaded from doing so by two senior Catholic barristers who told Sir Michael that the Northern Irish bar would see this as a snub.[21] Ironically, the comments of Lord Justice Gibson, acquitting the three officers and criticising the decision to prosecute them, might be seen as a snub to the Attorney-General.

215. We believe the decision whether or not to prosecute should never be influenced by political considerations. It would be equally wrong to prosecute as to refrain from prosecuting for reasons of political expediency.

216. Two further powers of the Attorney-General have concerned us. The first is his power to refer points of law of public importance to the higher courts for review. Following Lord Diplock's judgment in the *Attorney-General's Reference* (see para. 105 above), it appears that no useful purpose would be served by referring the recent acquittals by Mr Justice MacDermott and Lord Justice Gibson to any higher court. The second power is the Attorney-General's ability under the EPA to order that particular offences normally triable only in the Diplock Courts, should be tried by a jury.

217. The abolition of jury trial and the introduction of the Diplock Courts in 1973 was largely based on the premise that jurors would be intimidated by paramilitaries. In theory, at least, this jusitification should not apply in cases where members of the security forces are charged with murder or similar serious offences. Some lawyers who testified to us proposed that all such trials should be conducted with a jury. Such a solution would certainly help to absolve the judiciary from the suspicion that they are deliberately exonerating the security forces. However, a more serious objection is that this would help to confirm the impression already widely current that the security forces are subject to a different set of rules from other citizens.

218. The Director of Public Prosecutions (D.P.P.) is a civil servant, rather than a political appointee. He is responsible for reviewing evidence assembled by the police and for deciding whether or not to institute prosecutions. In a disturbing number of cases the D.P.P. has delayed for many months before deciding to institute proceedings against members of the security forces. Indeed, in the case of *Martin Malone* (see above, para. 50), the D.P.P. had been delaying his decision for six months at the time our Inquiry was held, even though statements from all civilian witnesses were given to the R.U.C. the day after the shooting. After we completed our hearings, the D.P.P. announced the prosecution of a member of the U.D.R. for the murder of Malone.

219. The Lord Chancellor, the highest judicial authority in the United Kingdom, and also a political appointee in the Government, has asserted that there are '*legitimate policy reasons*' for delaying the D.P.P.'s decision to prosecute. (Para. 171 above). We reject this view, first because the D.P.P. should be immune from political influence and secondly because it asserts cynically that it is more important to protect the security forces from adverse criticism than it is to serve the legitimate concerns of the family of the deceased, the community at large and, not least, the individual members of the security forces who linger under threat of possible murder charges for many months.

220. This policy has prevented Coroners from carrying out their statutory functions (see above, para. 170). Furthermore, it encourages the public perception that the security forces operate above or outside the law. In a number of cases considered by the Inquiry, there appears to be no other explanation of the conduct of the D.P.P.'s office than a desire to shield the R.U.C., U.D.R. or British Army from public criticism. (See e.g. the cases of *Seamus Grew* and *Roddy Carroll* (para. 54), *Eugene Toman, Gervase McKerr* and *Sean Burns* (para. 55), *Danny Barrett* (para. 67)). These cases contrast sharply with the speedy response of the D.P.P. for England and Wales over the shooting of Steven Waldorf.

221. We believe that the D.P.P. might seem to be unduly influenced by political considerations in deciding whether to prosecute members of the security forces for the unlawful use of firearms. We are also disturbed by the fact that the D.P.P. refuses to give reasons for not prosecuting, despite the recommendation in the British Government's Bennett Report that reasons should be given.[22] This refusal, together with excessive delays, reinforces the public perception that offences committed by members of the security forces are deliberately covered up.

222. As we state in our section on police investigations (paras. 146 *et seq.* above), we believe that a truly independent prosecuting authority is required in Northern Ireland. We agree with Boyle, Hadden, Greer and Walsh's submission to the Baker Enquiry into the PTA that the D.P.P.'s formal subordination to the Attorney-General should be removed. However, this alone will not guarantee his independence.

We believe that an independent prosecutor should be appointed to conduct a full investigation of any killing by a member of the security forces and to submit findings to the D.P.P. within 21 days. The D.P.P. should decide whether to prosecute within a further 7 days, thus enabling Coroners to open inquests within 28 days. The D.P.P. should always be required to give detailed reasons for the decision not to prosecute members of the security forces in such cases.

Finally, we believe that whatever difficulties may be encountered in dismantling the Diplock Courts and repealing the Emergency legislation, those difficulties must be overcome and jury trial must be restored before public confidence in the administration of justice can be established in Northern Ireland.

Notes

1. *Report of the Commission to consider legal procedures to deal with terrorist activities in Northern Ireland*, (Diplock Report) Cmnd. 5185, London 1972: Terms of Reference.

2. Northern Ireland (Emergency Provisions) Act 1978 (EPA), Section 31.

3. EPA, Section 2. In his *Review of the Operation of the Northern Ireland (Emergency Provisions) Act 1978*, (Baker Report), Cmnd. 9222, April 1984, Sir George Baker recommends redrafting this section to place the initial onus for opposing bail on the prosecution. (Para. 81).

4. Diplock Report, para. 90.

5. EPA, Section 8 (2). The Baker Report recommends redrafting this section to make clear that the judges retain discretion to exclude confessions and that violence and threat of violence are prohibited. (Para. 201 and Appendix J).

6. EPA, Section 9. The Baker Report recommends no change. (Para. 213).

7. EPA, Section 21. The Baker Report recommends no significant change. (Paras. 408 to 430).

8. EPA, Sections 12 and 33 (3)(c). The Baker Report recommends repeal of these sections. (Para. 236).

9. EPA, Sections 13, 15, 16, 17, 19 and 20. The Baker Report recommends no substantial change, except to insert 'reasonable' before 'suspicion' where relevant. (E.g. para. 303).

10. EPA, Sections 11, 13 and 14. The Baker Report recommends that 'reasonableness' be required for all arrests and searches without a warrant (paras. 283, 285, 346).

11. EPA, Sections 15 and 16.

12. EPA, Section 11., statistics from the Baker Report, para. 276.

13. Spencer S., *The Prevention of Terrorism Bill 1983*, October 1983, National Council for Civil Liberties, London. The Baker Report recommends amalgamating EPA Section 11 with PTA Section 12 for Northern Ireland. (Para. 267 & 300). The initial holding period would then be 48 hours, with a maximum further 5 day period authorised by the Secretary of State or one of his Junior Ministers. (Paras. 279 and 305).

14. PTA, Sections 3 to 9. For a recent detailed critique of these provisions, see Spencer S., *op. cit.*

15. Spencer S., *op. cit.*

16. PTA, Section 11.

17. Lord T. Gifford Q.C., *Supergrasses: The use of accomplice evidence in Northern Ireland*, 1984, Cobden Trust.

18. Spencer S., *op. cit.*

19. Boyle K., Hadden T., Hillyard P., *Law and State: The Case of Northern Ireland,* 1975 Martin Robertson, p. 12.

20. Harvey R., *Diplock and the Assault on Civil Liberties,* 1980, The Haldane Society, London, p. 28.

21. *Irish Times,* 9 June 1984.

22. *Report of the Committee of Inquiry into Police Interrogation Procedures in Northern Ireland,* (Bennett Report), Cmnd. 7497, March 1979, para. 379.

11. Conclusions and Recommendations

223. We are convinced by the evidence we have heard that public confidence in the security forces can only be maintained if the British Army and the Royal Ulster Constabulary are seen to be subject to the rule of law. We recognise that the security forces in Northern Ireland play a counter-insurgency role distinct from the methods of policing in other parts of Ireland and the United Kingdom. However, calls from political figures for the police and army to be given a 'free hand' in dealing with paramilitary violence are at best irresponsible; at worst, they create a climate of opinion that the law provides no restraints of any kind.

After careful consideration of all the evidence we conclude as follows:

General Findings

224. The number of civilians shot dead by the security forces in Northern Ireland is unacceptable. At least 155 of the 269 or more persons killed by the security forces since 1969 were civilians with no known connection to paramilitary organisations or activities. The failure of the British Government to curb these killings supports the view that a certain level of death, violence and public resentment is officially regarded as acceptable, on condition that it is primarily confined to one section of the community in Northern Ireland.

225. The law governing the use of deadly force by the police and army in Northern Ireland is inadequate. We find that judges in Northern Ireland and in the British House of Lords have interpreted the law in a manner which allows too much scope for members of the security forces. The attitude of some judges amounts virtually to endorsement of martial law. Internal Army and police instructions on the use of firearms are kept secret from the public and breaches of those instructions go unpunished.

226. The procedures for investigating questionable killings by the security forces are ineffective. Coroners' Inquests are unreasonably delayed and the scope of their inquiry is narrower than in the rest of the United Kingdom. We have heard evidence that the R.U.C. is incapable of conducting fair and impartial investigations into the conduct of any branch of the security forces. The Director of Public Prosecutions is subject to the political control of the Attorney-General, who is a member of the British Government, and we find that political considerations have influenced the decision whether or not to prosecute in a number of cases. We believe such influence to be improper.

227. The continuing failure of successive British Parliaments to bring domestic law into line with Article 6 (1) of the International Covenant on Civil and Political Rights and Article 2 of the European Convention on Human Rights and Fundamental Freedoms, to both of which the United Kingdom is a party, reflects an administrative policy and practice which seeks to place the security forces outside the law.

228. While the Nationalist (and predominantly Roman Catholic) community makes up approximately 40% of Northern Ireland's population, members of this community account for the vast majority of civilians killed by the security forces. By contrast, less than 10% of the security forces come from the Catholic community. We find that this community suffers disproportionately from the unrestrained use of firearms by the security forces and that Nationalists have become especially alienated from the administration of justice.

229. We conclude that the British Government has a clear and immediate duty to introduce legislation complying with the United Nations Covenant and the European Convention and to institute genuinely independent machinery for investigating and prosecuting unlawful killings by the security forces.

230. If the British Government fails or refuses to act, we believe that the Government of Ireland would be justified in referring Britain's violations of the European Convention in Northern Ireland to the European Commission on Human Rights in Strasbourg.

Specific Findings and Recommendations

231. We consider that the British Government in Northern Ireland has violated and continues to violate the international and domestic legal principle that every person's right to life must be protected by the law.

(1) The Criminal Law Act (Northern Ireland) 1967, Section 3 (1), is inadequate to ensure that lethal force is used only when absolutely necessary. (Paras. 91 to 145, and especially paras. 141 *et seq.*).

(2) The use of firearms to kill persons engaged in threats to property, as distinct from threats to life, cannot be justified. (See especially the *Farrell* case, paras. 114 to 122).

(3) Several senior judges, particularly Lord Diplock, Lord Justice Gibson and Mr Justice MacDermott, have made statements from the bench which imply that Northern Ireland is under a state of quasi-martial law. We accept the evidence we have received that such statements are fatal to public confidence in judicial impartiality, especially when they are considered against the background of an acquittal rate approaching 100% for members of the security forces charged with the unlawful use of firearms. We believe that these judges should not continue to adjudicate on cases arising under the emergency legislation (paras. 130 and 134-5).

(4) We received evidence that over 269 people have been shot by the security forces on duty in Northern Ireland between 1969 and March 1984. Over 150 of these killings, or 57%, are estimated as unarmed civilian casualties – people with no manifest connection to paramilitary organisations. In over 20 cases which we examined in detail it appears to us that more force was used than absolutely necessary (paras. 42-80).

We therefore conclude that at least 20 *prima facie* violations of Article 6 (1) of the United Nations International Covenant on Civil and Political Rights and of Article 2 of the European Convention for the Protection of Human Rights and Fundamental Freedoms have been committed by the security forces in Northern Ireland in the period in question (para. 145).

(5) Despite the high number of civilian casualties, we found that very few have led to prosecutions. When prosecutions were brought, the results were nearly always unconvincing. We received abundant evidence that public confidence in the evenhandedness of judicial administration has been gravely weakened by the apparent absence of any effective sanctions for the killing of innocent civilians (paras. 37-41).

(6) We recommend that Army and police instructions relating to the issue and use of firearms be made public. These instructions

should comply with the United Nations Covenant and the European Convention and should be given statutory force. Breaches of the instructions should be punishable under the criminal law and any serious breach should deprive a defendant of any 'good faith' or 'justification' defence to a charge of murder, manslaughter, unlawful wounding or any attempt to commit such offences (paras. 98-102).

232. We are convinced that many people in Northern Ireland believe there is no effective legal remedy for violations of the 'right to life' conferred by the International Covenant and the European Convention. This belief appears to stem from Britain's failure to legislate against killings by the security forces which do not fulfil the international law requirement of 'absolute necessity'. The absence of legal redress is further demonstrated by the absence of a truly independent police complaints procedure. We conclude that the denial of effective remedies violates Article 13 of the European Convention. (See para. 147 to 161 above).

(1) In the *Farrell* case (see paras. 112 to 120 above), the British House of Lords avoided its responsibility to determine the duty of care owed to civilians by members of the security forces. Northern Ireland courts have regularly held shootings by soldiers and police officers to be justified on grounds so broad and vague as to discourage families from bringing claims for damages. Although civil remedies are in theory available, we believe that the attitudes of the courts may well deter bereaved families from suing the security forces.

(2) We have been told of cases where the British Government has offered trivial sums in settlement of wrongful death claims against the Ministry of Defence. (See the *McElhone* case (£3,000), para. 53 above, and the *Maura Meehan* case (£1,200), para. 69 above). In our view, such sums as these are not 'effective remedies' within the meaning of Article 13 of the European Convention.

(3) There is no effective or adequate complaints procedure to deal with civilian grievances against members of the security forces in Northern Ireland. We are satisfied that many justified grievances are not pursued because there is no confidence in a fair adjudication. Although the British Government announced a review of the complaints system in November 1981, no proposals have yet been published. By contrast, the Government appears determined to implement its proposals in the rest of the United Kingdom. Public con-

fidence in the security forces can only be restored by the establishment of an effective complaints procedure which is demonstrably impartial and independent of control by the security forces. (Para. 154 to 160).

(4) We recommend that an independent board or commission be established on which all communities in Northern Ireland would be represented, together with members of the security forces. This body should have the power to review policy matters, including the use of force. It should have the power to adjudicate on police misconduct, to subpoena witnesses and issue findings and recommendations for immediate specific action. Where the security forces oppose any recommendation, a final adjudicating body should be empowered to enforce decisions where appropriate. (Para. 158, 159).

233. A democratic government has a duty to protect all within its jurisdiction from breaches of the law, whether committed by civilians or by its security forces. The British Government has failed to protect the people of Northern Ireland. No adequate machinery exists to investigate, prosecute or punish wrongs committed by members of the security forces. Its absence inevitably weakens respect for the law in Northern Ireland.

(1) The public perceives the Coroners' Courts as the principal forum for establishing the causes and circumstances of death. However, these courts have lost their effectiveness due to:

(a) unwarranted delays in holding inquests; the Government admits some inquests are delayed for 'policy reasons' (see para. 171 above);

(b) Inadequate inquiry into causes and circumstances of death; material witnesses are not summoned and unreliable scientific evidence has been accepted (see paras. 174 to 181 above);

(c) Unsatisfactory 'findings'; juries in Northern Ireland have more limited powers than in England and Wales because they may not bring in a verdict of 'unlawful killing', they are restricted to recording 'findings' and they may not recommend measures to avoid similar deaths in future (see paras. 182, 183 above).

(d) The exclusion of families and other properly interested persons from effective participation in the inquest (see paras. 178 to 180 above).

(2) We therefore recommend that:

(a) The Coroner must be under a duty to open the inquest forthwith when a death is reported;

(b) Unless a person is charged within 28 days with causing the death, no adjournment beyond this period should be permitted;

(c) An inquest should always be held with a jury when a death is suspected to have been caused by a member of the security forces;

(d) The security forces should play no role in jury selections. The Coroner's officer should receive a list of randomly selected jurors and summon them in strict order.

(e) The Coroner should require the attendance of all members of the security forces who may have relevant evidence and the security forces should be obliged to inform the Coroner of the identities of all such persons;

(f) There should be no power to exempt from attendance any witness served with a summons, but witnesses should continue to enjoy the privilege against self-incrimination;

(g) Documentary evidence should be inadmissible unless the Coroner is satisfied that there is good and sufficient reason why the maker of the document cannot attend;

(h) The Coroner should be obliged to examine all who wish to tender evidence;

(i) Properly interested persons should be entitled to call relevant evidence before the jury and to address the jury on the facts and on the lawfulness or otherwise of the killing;

(j) Properly interested persons should be entitled to Legal Aid to secure legal representation and to obtain independent forensic scientific or autopsy reports;

(k) Police reports and witness statements should be disclosed to properly interested persons;

(l) The jury should be entitled to record a verdict of 'unlawful killing', as in England and Wales;

(m) The jury's right to add recommendations for avoiding similar deaths in future should be restored.

(3) We accept the evidence presented to us that the Attorney-General takes account of political considerations in deciding whether to prosecute members of the security forces for the unlawful use of their firearms. We believe that it is no more justifiable to decline to prosecute for political reasons than it would be to bring a prosecution for such reasons (para. 215).

(4) We heard complaints of the way in which Crown counsel conducted prosecutions of members of the security forces. Although no trial transcripts were available, we find some support for these criticisms in the Attorney-General's failure to conduct any Northern

Ireland prosecution, by contrast with his leading the prosecution of the London police officers charged in the *Waldorf* case (see para. 213 above).

We recommend that the Attorney-General should demonstrate the British Government's commitment to equal justice in all parts of the United Kingdom by prosecuting members of the security forces in person.

(5) We believe that the Director of Public Prosecutions for Northern Ireland has further weakened public confidence in his impartiality by declining to state reasons for refusing to prosecute. The D.P.P. has repeatedly delayed Coroners' inquests by apparently failing to consider police investigations into killings by the security forces within a reasonable time (paras. 218-221)

We recommend that the D.P.P. should be required by law to give full and adequate reasons both for a decision not to prosecute members of the security forces for killing civilians and for any delay beyond 28 days in deciding whether to prosecute.

(6) We received evidence that delays had often occurred in police investigations into killings by members of the security forces. Sometimes families were told by members of the R.U.C. that the police could not investigate a killing by a soldier. We consider that the present system, in which the R.U.C. investigate both themselves and other branches of the security forces, is wholly inadequate (paras. 146-153).

If public confidence is to be restored in the investigation process, then a genuinely independent prosecutor's office must be created, comparable with the Procurator Fiscal in Scotland or the Special Prosecutor in the United States. The independent prosecutor should be required to report to the D.P.P. within 21 days of the death and to give sufficient reasons for any delay beyond such time. The D.P.P. should decide within 7 days whether to bring a prosecution or give sufficient reasons for not doing so (para. 222).

(7) We recommend that all persons charged with an arrestable offence in Northern Ireland, including members of the security forces, be tried by a judge and jury and not by a judge sitting alone in a Diplock Court. The justification originally advanced for eliminating the jury was the danger that paramilitary groups whose members were on trial might intimidate the jury. However, Coroners' courts continue to sit with juries and we have seen no evidence to substantiate the existence of any continuing threat to jurors.

The Diplock Courts are understandably seen as a symbol of injustice by a substantial section of the community. Jury trial is a fundamental guarantee of the rule of law and is so recognised in the United States and many Commonwealth countries, as well as in the United Kingdom. We do not feel that public confidence can be achieved unless jury trial is restored.

(8) We were disturbed by statements made recently in open court by Mr Justice MacDermott and Lord Justice Gibson, when they were acquitting members of the R.U.C. charged with murder (see paras. 54 and 55). These statements imply judicial support for the summary execution of suspects. It is difficult to see how public confidence in the impartiality of the judiciary can exist while these judges continue to try cases arising under the emergency legislation.

Part of the programme necessary for restoring public confidence in the administration of justice in Northern Ireland should be a Judicial Services Commission, which might also provide a complaints machinery to deal with breaches of judicial standards of conduct. The Commission, for which a precedent can be found in the constitution proposed by the British Government for Zimbabwe, would review all proposed judicial appointments and screen applicants for their competence, impartiality and integrity.

(9) The British Government has in recent years failed to take suitably vigorous action to prevent civilian deaths in Northern Ireland at the hands of the security forces. For example:

(a) Since direct rule began in 1972, no official public inquiry into killings by the security forces has been commissioned by the British Parliament. Yet, between 1968 and 1972, four major official inquiries examined alleged improprieties and killir.gs by the security forces (paras. 29-36).

(b) 14 killings by rubber and plastic bullets have been considered by the United Nations Human Rights Commission's Sub-Committee on the Prevention of Discrimination and Protection of Minorities, by the European Parliament and by the European Commission on Human Rights, as well as by independent international tribunals (paras. 71-81).

No prosecution has been brought for any breach of Army Rules of Engagement for PVC Baton Rounds (para. 78).

In August 1984, following the 15th death, that of John Downes, the British Government once again refused to conduct an official public inquiry (paras. 73-75).

(c) The reaction of the British Home Secretary to the near-fatal shootings by the Metropolitan Police in London recently is in sharp contrast to the Government's silence on civilian deaths in Northern Ireland: he immediately assured Parliament that internal police inquiries and a review of police instructions on the issue and use of firearms would take place (para. 101)

(10) We do not believe that, at this late stage, any official Government tribunal would restore public confidence in Northern Ireland. Only by vigorous action, such as we recommend, can that confidence be regained. As a first step, plastic bullets, which are both lethal and unpredictable, should be outlawed.

(11) We are disturbed by the refusal of the Government to answer questions of vital public importance to the people of Northern Ireland. For example, we do not accept that statistics on numbers of members of the security forces charged and convicted for criminal matters in Northern Ireland 'could be obtained only at disproportionate cost' (see para. 20).

234. We reject the view that different legal standards may be applied to the conduct of the security forces in Northern Ireland from those applied in the rest of Ireland and the United Kingdom. We disagree with Lord Diplock's claim (see para. 109 above) that the legal rights and duties of a soldier should be more than those of an ordinary citizen. We are driven to conclude that a primary cause of the violence against civilians with which this report is concerned is the failure to train soldiers in policing techniques.

(1) We recommend fresh legislation defining the limits on the permissible use of lethal force in accordance with the International Covenant and the European Convention. We recognise that a soldier's duties will call for life and death decisions which a civilian rarely, if ever, will have to make. However, unless soldiers can be trained in the responsible exercise of their duties under domestic and international law, then the British Government must take the responsibility for deciding whether its Army is appropriately employed in Northern Ireland.

(2) We found the role of the U.D.R. in Northern Ireland particularly worrying. Members are recruited almost exclusively from the Unionist community. We understand that it is the only regiment in the British Army which is never posted abroad and is employed to garrison and patrol its members' home territory. As such, the U.D.R. is perceived as a sectarian vigilante force by Nationalists (paras. 45 and 50).

We believe that the U.D.R. as presently constituted endangers public confidence in the security forces as a whole. The British Government has the responsibility for disbanding it.

235. The evidence we have heard leads us to conclude that an administrative practice has been allowed to develop in Northern Ireland, by which killings in violation of the European Convention and the International Covenant are at least tolerated, if not actually encouraged. Undercover units of the British Army and the R.U.C. are trained to shoot to kill even where killing is not legally justifiable and where alternative tactics could and should be used. Such administrative practices are illegal in domestic and international law. They should be stopped and training for them should be discontinued immediately (paras. 54 and 55).

236. In conclusion, we find that the misuse of firearms by the security forces in Northern Ireland is part of a broader pattern of human rights violations which has led to a serious breakdown in public confidence in the security forces and in the administration of justice generally. Unless this problem is confronted with determination by a British Government committed to restoring public confidence in the rule of law, we fear that violations will continue and may even spread to other parts of the United Kingdom.

We consider that the Government of Ireland, as a party to the European Convention, would be justified in bringing an interstate application to the European Commission on Human Rights under Article 24 of the Convention, alleging violations of Article 2 and Article 13.

Appendix A

Civilians Shot Dead in Disputed Circumstances by Members of the Security Forces in Northern Ireland

This list is compiled from information submitted to our Inquiry by the Irish Information Partnership, by Mr Steven C. Greer and by the Association for Legal Justice.

We recognise that there may be disputes about the categorising of some cases since official explanations frequently differ from those of local eyewitnesses. However, we believe it is important to publish the most accurate information available and we hope others will carry out further research in the interests of greater accuracy. Given the disputed circumstances of these deaths, it is inevitable that certain people listed as 'civilians' may, in fact, have been paramilitaries. We have adopted the Irish Information Partnership's definition of 'civilian' (see Report, para. 22) but we have also included some acknowledged members of paramilitary groups where evidence suggests they were killed in circumstances which may not have justified the use of deadly force.

NAME	SUMMARY	DATE	AGENT	CATEGORY	PLACE
John Gallagher	Shot by B Specials dispersing assembly. Scarman report found: 'no justification for the shooting'.	14/8/69	BSpec	Street rally	Armagh
Samuel McLarnon	Shot in sitting room by RUC bullet during street gunbattle Scarman report: 'innocent victim'.	14/8/69	RUC	Street disturbance	Ardoyne, North Belfast
Michael Lynch	Shot in street by RUC, trying to avoid riot. Scarman said: innocent bystander.	14/8/69	RUC	'Riot'	Ardoyne, North Belfast
Hugh McCabe (Trooper)	British Army ('BA') soldier on leave shot while lying on balcony in Divis Flats by RUC marksman. Scarman rept: 'innocent victim'.	14/9/69	RUC	Street disturbance	West Belfast

NAME	SUMMARY	DATE	AGENT	CATEGORY	PLACE
Patrick Rooney	9 yrs, in bedroom in Divis Flats. RUC sprayed area with machine-gun mounted on armoured car. Scarman rept: firing 'not justified'.	14/9/69	RUC	Street disturbance	West Belfast
George Dickie	Shot by BA on Shankill Rd after Hunt Report proposed disbanding B Specials.	11/11/69	BA	'Riot'	Shankill, North Belfast
Herbert Hawe	Shot in circumstances similar to above	11/11/69	BA	'Riot'	North Belfast
Patrick Elliman	Elderly man in street wearing slippers: shot by BA sniper during army-imposed curfew Died one week later.	3/7/70	BA	'Falls Curfew'	West Belfast
William Burns	Shot by BA in Falls Curfew while chatting to neighbours	3/7/70	BA	'Falls Curfew'	West Belfast
Charles O'Neill	Shot by BA in Falls Curfew.	3/7/70	BA	'Falls Curfew'	West Belfast
Zbigniew Uglik	Londoner on holiday shot by BA sniper while climbing over wall to get camera from his hotel. Army 'thought he was a gunman'.	4/7/70	BA	'Falls Curfew'	West Belfast
Daniel O'Hagan	Shot by BA in confrontation with crowd in New Lodge Road. (Local residents said he was unarmed.)	31/7/70	BA	'Riot'	North Belfast
Bernard Watt	Shot by BA in riot: Hooker St., Ardoyne	7/2/71	BA	'Riot'	North Belfast
William Halligan	Shot by BA marksman in Balaclava St.	5/3/71	BA	'Riot'	West Belfast
Seamus Cusack	Shot by BA in riot: Army claimed C had a rifle; civilian witnesses denied this.	8/7/71	BA	'Riot'	Derry City
Desmond Beattie	Shot by BA as above; Army claimed B had a nail-bomb; Lord Gifford, English barrister, held unofficial inquiry: found C & B not armed.	8/7/71	BA	'Riot'	Derry City
Harry Thornton	Shot by BA when his van backfired by RUC Barracks, Springfield Road.	7/8/71	BA	'Riot'	West Belfast

NAME	SUMMARY	DATE	AGENT	CATEGORY	PLACE
Frank McGuinness	15 yr-old shot by BA while watching soldier dismantling a bomb during anti-internment riots.	9/8/71	BA	'Riot'	West Belfast
Desmond Healey	14 yr-old shot by BA in Andersonstown during anti-internment riots.	9/8/71	BA	'Riot'	West Belfast
Sarah Worthington	Shot by BA who entered her home believing it empty. BA spokesman at Inquest acknowledged mistake.	9/8/71	BA	'Accident'	North Belfast
Leo McGuigan	Shot by BA on Crumlin Rd.	9/8/71	BA	'Riot'	North Belfast
Noel Philips	Shot by BA in Ballymurphy in anti-internment riots.	9/8/71	BA	'Riot'	West Belfast
Daniel Taggart	Shot by BA in Ballymurphy as above.	9/8/71	BA	'Riot'	West Belfast
Joan Connolly	Shot by BA in Ballymurphy while going for help to R.U.C. station.	9/8/71	BA	'Riot'	West Belfast
Norman Watson	Shot by BA in Armagh while trying to remove car at roadblock.	9/8/71	BA	'Accident'	North Armagh
Fr Hugh Mullan	Shot by BA while trying to give last rites to dying man in Ballymurphy.	9/8/71	BA	'Riot'	West Belfast
John Beattie	Shot on Springfield Rd by BA, who claimed he was driving van being used as cover by snipers.	9/8/71	BA	'Riot'	West Belfast
Edward Doherty	Shot by BA on Whiterock Rd.	9/8/71	BA	'Riot'	West Belfast
William Ferris	Shot at Crumlin Road roadblock by BA, who acknowledged mistake. Family recovered £14,500 compensation.	10/8/71	BA	'Accident'	North Belfast
John Lavery	Shot in New Lodge Rd by BA, who claimed he was armed. Soldier's statement not taken till July 72; Inquest (Oct 72) told no evidence of gun was found.	11/8/71	BA	'Accident'	North Belfast
William McKavana	Shot by BA in Markets on suspicion of being armed.	11/8/71	BA	'Accident'	Central Belfast

NAME	SUMMARY	DATE	AGENT	CATEGORY	PLACE
Eamonn McDevitt	Deaf-mute shot by BA while holding a toy pistol in Strabane.	18/8/71	BA	'Riot'	West Tyrone
Hugh Heron	No further details on Irish Information Partnership's file.	19/8/71	BA	'Accident'	West Belfast
Joseph Corr	Shot by BA in Bally-murphy.	29/8/71	BA	'Crossfire/ Gun-battle.'	West Belfast
Annette McGavigan	14yr-old shot by BA in crossfire in Derry	6/9/71	BA	'Accident'	Derry City
Wm. McGreanery	Shot by BA in Derry. Inquest was told he was shot walking in street with others.	14/9/71	BA	'Accident'	Derry City
David Thompson	Shot by BA in Bally-macarret area. Inquest (Oct.72) was told he was unarmed.	17/10/71	BA	'Crossfire/ Gun-battle.'	East Belfast
Maura Meehan	Shot by BA together with her sister (IRA member) Dorothy Mc-Guire, travelling in car. (See Report, para. 69)	23/10/71	BA	'Accident'	West Belfast
James McLaughlin Sean Ruddy Robert Anderson	Shot by BA in unarmed robbery attempt in Newry. (See Report, para. 114: The Farrell Activity Case).	23/10/71	BA	Non-Political Criminal Activity.	South Down
Michael McLarnon	Shot by BA while standing in doorway of his own home. Soldier wrote to family and said he was sorry.	29/10/71	BA	'Crossfire/ Gun-battle.'	North Belfast
John Copeland	Died in hospital from wounds received in above incident. Inquest (2/11/73) was told he was unarmed.	30/10/71	BA	'Crossfire/ Gun-battle.'	North Belfast
Christopher Quinn	Shot by BA while on a vigilante patrol in Unity Flats.	3/11/71	BA	'Accident'	Central Belfast
Kathleen Thompson	Shot by BA in her own back garden. (See Report, para.58).	6/11/71	BA	'Accident'	Derry City
Joseph Parker	Shot in dance hall in Ardoyne by BA during search and melée. Two years later his widow received £12,000 compensation.	12/11/71	BA	'Riot'	North Belfast

NAME	SUMMARY	DATE	AGENT	CATEGORY	PLACE
Martin McShane	Youth shot by BA machine-gun while holding a toy gun at a children's soccer match at Coalisland. Judge dismissed claim for damages in Jan. 1975.	14/12/71	BA	'Accident'	East Tyrone
Joseph Ward	Shot by BA in N. Queen Street. BA acknowledged accidental discharge by sentry	12/1/72	BA	'Accident'	North Belfast
Jack Duddy Patrick Doherty Hugh Gilmore Bernard McGuigan John Young Michael McDaid William Nash Michael Kelly Kevin McElhinney James Wray Gerald McKinney Gerald Donaghy William McKinney	'Bloody Sunday'. All were killed during largely peaceful anti-internment rally. Army claimed all of dead or wounded were gunmen or petrol- or nail-bombers. All civilian witnesses including many British, Irish & foreign journalists, said none of the dead or wounded had a gun or bomb. (See Report paras. 28 & 34).	30/1/72	BA	Deliberate Shooting	Derry City
Thomas McIlhoy	Shot by BA near own home in Ballymurphy. Coroner said: 'innocent sufferer' at Inquest (Dec. 1972).	2/2/72	BA	'Accident'	West Belfast
Michael Connors John Mahon (Maughan)	Itinerants together in car, shot by RUC for failing to stop. Inquest April 73.	1/3/72	BA	Non-Political Criminal Activity.	West Belfast
Patrick Magee	Student shot by BA on Falls Road while running to church for shelter as BA were firing from several hundred yards away when there was a riot following BA shooting of unarmed I.R.A. leader Joe McCann	17/4/72	BA	'Riot'	West Belfast
Patrick Donaghey	Pensioner shot in chest while in his flat in Divis Flats during BA shooting following killing of Joe McCann (see above)	23/4/72	BA	'Riot'	West Belfast
Francis Rowntree	11yr-old shot in head with rubber bullet by BA at point blank range, as he emerged	23/4/72	BA	'Riot'	Central Belfast

NAME	SUMMARY	DATE	AGENT	CATEGORY	PLACE
Francis Rowntree (cont.),	from Divis Flats. Surgeon confirmed injuries consistent with eyewitness accounts.				
Patrick McVeigh	Shot by BA Special Patrol while on unarmed vigilante patrol in district. Inquest (Dec. 1972) heard that RUC only learned of BA involvement the following day.	12/5/72	BA	Covert Military Operation	West Belfast
Joseph Campbell	17 yr-old shot by BA in Ardoyne.	11/6/72	BA	Unclassified	North Belfast
Norman McGrath	Shot by BA in crossfire of gun-battle. No evidence that he was armed.	11/6/72	BA	'Crossfire/ Gun-battle.'	North Belfast
James Bonnar	Shot by BA at Whiterock Rd. Army claim he failed to stop at road block. Inquest 8/10/73 found 'death by misadventure.'	25/6/72	BA	Deliberate Shooting	West Belfast
Fr Noel Fitzpatrick	Shot by BA trying to give last rites to dying person.	9/7/72	BA	'Accident'	West Belfast
John Mooney	Shot by BA at Ligoniel. Inquest (May 73) was told he was searched by BA then shot at close range shortly after. Coroner said: 'It looks unlikely that we will ever get satisfactorily to the bottom of this'.	14/7/72	BA	Military Operation	North Belfast
Tobias Molloy	Shot at point blank range by BA with rubber bullet when riot broke out with Army at border checkpoint. Molloy was in Official IRA.	16/7/72	BA	Military Operation	East Tyrone
Francis McKeown	Shot by BA when trying to move roadblock to gain access to home.	16/7/72	BA	'Accident'	West Belfast
James Casey	Shot by BA while driving car.	24/7/72	BA	'Crossfire/ Gun-battle.'	Derry City
Daniel Hegarty	Shot during 'Operation Motorman' (removal of I.R.A. 'No-go' barriers). Killed in presence of cousin who gave eyewitness account.	31/7/72	BA	'Crossfire/ Gun-battle.'	Derry City

NAME	SUMMARY	DATE	AGENT	CATEGORY	PLACE
Robert McKinney	Shot by BA at Shankill Rd. roadblock.	7/9/72	BA	'Accident'	North Belfast
Robert Johnson	As above. Inquest (Oct. 72) was told by counsel for Dept. of Home Affairs: 'Deceased were innocent persons tragically killed in situations over which they had no control'. No evidence of any disciplinary action.	7/9/72	BA	'Accident'	North Belfast
Michael Quigley	Shot by BA in Derry. No evidence he was armed.	17/9/72	BA	'Crossfire/ Gun-battle.'	Derry City
Daniel Rooney	Shot by plain clothes soldiers on Donegall Rd. BA claimed R and friend opened fire on plain clothes patrol. Civilian witnesses denied any shooting prior to shots from BA car.	27/9/72	BA	Covert Military Operation	West Belfast
John Kelly	Shot 3 days before by BA, who claimed gun went off accidentally in struggle. Eyewitnesses said there was no struggle.	30/9/72	BA	'Accident'	West Belfast
Michael Hayes	Shot by BA on way home from social at school in West Belfast. BA made series of conflicting reports, claiming group of men acted suspiciously and one man produced a gun. No gun found on or near H. Jury returned open verdict in Dec. 1973.	1/10/72	BA	Deliberate Shooting	North Belfast
Alex Moorehead	Deaf youth shot by UDR patrol, who claimed he failed to stop when ordered. Youth's uncle in command of patrol.	7/10/72	UDR	'Accident'	West Tyrone
William Bell	Housing Executive employee shot by BA while working in Ardoyne. BA issued an apology.	5/12/72	BA	'Accident'	North Belfast
Joseph Ward	Shot by BA in N. Queen Street. BA acknowledged accidental discharge by sentry.	12/1/73	BA	'Accident'	North Belfast

NAME	SUMMARY	DATE	AGENT	CATEGORY	PLACE
Eliz. McGregor	Shot by BA in Ardoyne. BA acknowledged error but said shooting at a group of 4 men. Coroner told Inquest jury (Apr. 74) to return open verdict if not satisfied with BA explanation. Jury: 'Open Verdict'.	12/1/73	BA	'Accident'	North Belfast
Ambrose Hardy	Shot by BA during gun battle while waving a white flag in New Lodge Road area.	3/2/73	BA	'Crossfire/ Gun-battle.'	North Belfast
Brendan Maguire	Shot by BA in similar incident to Hardy. Belfast Magistrates Court awarded parents £2,583 compensation, Sept. 73.	3/2/73	BA	'Crossfire/ Gun-battle.'	North Belfast
Sean Loughran	Shot by BA in same incident. Family received £6,500 compensation after inquest (December 1975).	3/2/73	BA	'Crossfire/ Gun-battle.'	North Belfast
Joseph Sloan	Shot by BA in same incident as above.	3/2/73	BA	'Crossfire/ Gun-battle.'	North Belfast
James McCann	Shot by BA in same incident as above.	3/2/73	BA	'Crossfire/ Gun-battle.'	North Belfast
Hugh Connolly	Probably shot by BA in exchange gunfire at IRA funeral.	7/2/73	BA	'Crossfire/ Gun-battle.'	West Belfast
Kevin Heatley	12yr-old shot by BA in Newry. First criminal charge brought against BA member – Cpl. Foxford – (See Report para. 37/8).	28/2/73	BA	'Accident'	South Down
Edward Sharpe	Shot by BA sentry while standing at own door in Ardoyne.	13/3/73	BA	'Crossfire/ Gun-battle.'	North Belfast
Samuel Martin	Shot by BA returning to home near Newtownhamilton RUC barracks. Soldier charged with manslaughter; acquitted in Sept. 1974.	26/3/73	BA	'Accident'	South Armagh
Edward O'Rawe	Shot by BA who claimed he tried to escape BA search in Lower Falls. Unarmed, no evidence of paramilitary connection.	12/4/73	BA	Deliberate Shooting	West Belfast

NAME	SUMMARY	DATE	AGENT	CATEGORY	PLACE
Michael Leonard	County Donegal farmer shot by RUC when failed to stop at road block.	17/5/73	RUC	Non-Political Criminal Activity.	Central Belfast
Robert McIntyre	Shot by UDR when tried to hijack car in Shankill Rd.	19/5/73	UDR	Non-Political Criminal Activity.	North Belfast
Thomas Friel	Shot 17/5/73 by BA with rubber bullet in head, at range of 25 to 30 yds. BA claimed F was 'leading rioter'; F's brother Seamus said disturbances had ended some time earlier.	22/5/73	BA	Deliberate Shooting	Derry City
Anthony Mitchell	Shot by BA on Springfield Rd. BA issued conflicting reports; local people said M was drunk. Private Ross acquitted of murder by Judge MacDermott after evidence that he shot at distance of 2 yards in shadow.	12/6/73	BA	'Accident'	West Belfast
Robert McGuinness	Shot by BA (22/6/73). No evidence McG was armed.	26/6/73	BA	'Crossfire/ Gun-battle.'	Derry City
Joseph Walker	Shot by BA in taxi alleged to have been stolen. No evidence that he was armed.	3/12/73	BA	'Crossfire/ Gun-battle.'	Derry City
Alex Howell	Shot in Shankill Rd. following affray outside pub. L/Cpl Nicoll acquitted of unlawful killing (Dec. 74).	28/12/73	BA	'Riot'	North Belfast
Matilda Worthington	Elderly woman shot by BA returning fire after ambush on RAF at Newcastle.	29/1/74	BA	'Crossfire/ Gun-battle.'	North Belfast
Gary Reid (and one UDA member).	Shot on Newtownards Rd. by BA during riots. Inquest (Jan.75) found: 'Evidence suggests that the two dead men were not gunmen'. (UDA man not included in Irish Information Partnership statistics because a paramilitary)	15/2/74	BA	'Riot'	East Belfast
Daniel Burke	Shot by BA at Andersonstown Social Club.	9/4/74	BA	'Crossfire/ Gun-battle.'	West Belfast

NAME	SUMMARY	DATE	AGENT	CATEGORY	PLACE
William McDonald	Shot (13/4/74) by BA in riots on Shankill Road.	14/4/74	BA	'Riot'	North Belfast
Patrick Joe Cunningham	Educationally sub-normal youth shot by BA who claimed he ran away from patrol.	15/6/74	BA	Deliberate Shooting	East Tyrone
Hugh Devine	Shot by BA in Strabane. Soldier charged: no details of outcome.	22/6/74	BA	'Accident'	West Tyrone
Charles Irvine	Shot by BA in Falls Rd area. BA claimed returning fire at occupants of car: local witnesses said car backfired. No weapons found.	13/7/75	BA	'Accident'	West Belfast
Patrick McElhone	Shot by BA on family farm. (See Report, paras 53, 101, 105-113).	13/7/75	BA	Deliberate Shooting	Tyrone
Stephen Geddis	10yr-old shot (Aug 28) in head by BA with plastic bullet. Witnesses said G was an onlooker at group of 7 to 13yr-olds who had set cushions on fire and thrown stones at soldiers.	30/8/75	BA	'Riot'	West Belfast
Leo Norney	17yr-old shot by BA while crossing waste ground. BA claimed N was a gunman but no weapons were found. BA searched N's house but did not tell N's parents he was dead. Coroners' Inquest cleared N. BA apologised for shooting an innocent man.	14/9/75	BA	Deliberate Shooting	West Belfast
Hugh Woodside	Shot by BA in fracas during search of Long Bar in Shankill Rd.	31/1/76	BA	'Riot'	North Belfast
Rory Hawkins	Shot by BA during affray outside drinking club. Died after 2 wks.	26/4/76	BA	'Riot'	East Belfast
Anthony Gallagher	Shot by BA while travelling on bus. Prvt Scott charged and acquitted.	17/5/76	BA	'Accident'	Derry City
Liam Prince	Schoolteacher shot by BA at checkpoint. (See Report, para. 51)	12/6/76	BA	'Accident'	South Armagh

NAME	SUMMARY	DATE	AGENT	CATEGORY	PLACE
Majella O'Hare	12yr-old girl shot by BA machine gun. BA at first claimed she was shot by gunman, later claimed she was killed in crossfire.	14/8/76	BA	'Accident'	South Armagh
Brian Stewart	13yr-old shot (Oct 4) by BA who claimed he was leading a riot of 400 youths. Eyewitnesses & TV crews said no riot took place and S had only left home a few minutes before. S's mother took case to the European Commission of Human Rights, who admitted jurisdiction but ruled (Oct 1984) that plastic bullets do not violate Article 2 (right to life) of the European Convention.	10/10/76	BA	'Riot'	West Belfast
Patrick McGeown	Shot by BA when they opened fire on a pub.	15/12/76	BA	'Crossfire/ Gun-battle.'	South Armagh
John Joe Savage	Shot by BA travelling in hijacked car which failed to stop at roadblock.	18/12/76	BA	Non-Political Criminal Activity	West Belfast
Paul Kerr	Shot by RUC attempting burglary at Dungannon. RUC initially claimed gun-battle but later withdrew allegation.	27/12/76	RUC	Non-Political Criminal Activity	Tyrone
Wm. Strathearn	Shopkeeper shot at own door in Ahoghill when answering early morning call. Off-duty RUC member charged & convicted.	19/4/77	RUC	Assassination at own home	Antrim
Jack McCartan	Shot by BA in back on leaving Andersonstown Social Club of which he was manager. BA claimed a shot was fired at them and they replied with a single round. RUC said they recovered bullet & that forensic tests showed McCartan not killed by BA bullet. After RUC search, Fr Faul found another slug	4/8/77	BA	Deliberate Shooting	West Belfast

NAME	SUMMARY	DATE	AGENT	CATEGORY	PLACE
Jack McCartan (cont.)	embedded in door & gave it to RUC to examine. Civilian witnesses said there was no shooting before McC was killed.	4/8/77	BA	Deliberate Shooting	West Belfast
Dennis Neill	Shot by BA who claimed he was hijacking & burning a bus. Family denied BA allegations.	24/10/77	BA	'Riot'	West Belfast
Colm McNutt	Shot by plainclothes BA in Willam St, Derry. Army claimed he tried to hijack an unmarked military car. Civilian witnesses said he was shot on street without warning.	12/12/77	BA	Deliberate Shooting	Derry City
Paul Duffy	Shot by BA undercover unit lying in wait at IRA arms dump. BA said he was shot trying to escape – republican sources said he was shot without warning. They later admitted he was 'on active service'.	26/2/78	BA	Undercover Military Operation	East Tyrone
John Collins	Shot by BA travelling in hijacked car.	7/5/78	BA	Non-Political Criminal Activity.	West Belfast
Denis Heaney	Shot by BA who claimed he tried to hijack an unmarked military car. Civilian witnesses said he was shot on street without warning. (See Report, para. 61)	10/6/78	BA	Undercover Military Operation	Derry City
Billy Hanna James Mulvenna Jackie Mealy Denis Brown	Shot by BA in ambush on IRA bombing unit. Hanna was innocent passer-by; M, M & B were on a bombing mission but republican sources said they were shot without warning, not in exchange of fire as alleged by BA.	20/6/78	BA	Undercover Military Operation	North Belfast
John Boyle	16yr-old shot by BA lying in wait at IRA arms dump which had been notified to RUC by B's father. B had	11/7/78	BA	Undercover Military Operation	North Armagh

NAME	SUMMARY	DATE	AGENT	CATEGORY	PLACE
John Boyle (cont.)	returned to see if gun had been removed. 2 S.A.S. soldiers were charged with B's murder but acquitted by Lowry, L.C.J. on grounds that they reasonably feared B was a terrorist who was about to lift the gun and fire at the concealed patrol.	11/7/78	BA	Undercover Military Operation	North Armagh
James Taylor	Shot by BA while out wildfowling. Tyres on his car were slashed by BA patrol who then shot him when he asked for explanation. BA later admitted error; no prosecutions.	30/9/78	BA	Undercover Military Operation	East Tyrone
Patrick Duffy	Shot by BA at IRA arms dump. (See Report, para.62)	25/11/78	BA	Undercover Military Operation	Derry City
Doreen McGuinness	Shot by BA travelling in stolen car in Falls.	1/1/80	BA	Non-Political Criminal Activity	West Belfast
Paul Moan	Shot by BA after crashing through road-block in stolen car in Lower Falls.	31/3/80	BA	Non-Political Criminal Activity	West Belfast
Theresa Donaghey	Shot by BA travelling in car at border checkpoint in Strabane. Pvt. Robert Reid Davidson found guilty of manslaughter (See Report, para. 40).	12/4/80	BA	'Accident'	West Tyrone
Michael McCartan	16yr-old shot by RUC while painting slogans on wall in Ormeau Rd. RUC claimed they thought his paintbrush was a gun. RUC later apologised – no prosecutions.	23/7/80	RUC	'Accident'	South Belfast
Michael Donnelly	Social worker shot by BA with plastic bullet. D walking home, not involved in riot when hit according to witnesses.	10/8/80	BA	'Riot'	West Belfast
Jim Bell	Shot by BA outside Cookstown Hotel on suspicion of breaking & entering.	14/8/80	BA	Non-Political Criminal Activity.	West Belfast

NAME	SUMMARY	DATE	AGENT	CATEGORY	PLACE
Patrick McNally	Shot by UDR patrol on Lower Falls while joyriding in stolen car.	20/3/81	UDR	Non-Political Criminal Activity.	West Belfast
Paul Whitters	15yr-old shot by RUC with plastic bullet in head at 15-16 foot range. W was part of group of youths stoning RUC in hunger-strike riots on Apr.15. Died 10 days later.	25/4/81	RUC	'Riot'	Derry City
Julie Livingstone	14yr-old shot with plastic bullet from passing BA armoured personnel carrier. She was walking past peaceful anti-H Block protest when hit.	13/5/81	BA	Demonstration	West Belfast
Carol Ann Kelly	12yr-old shot with plastic bullet by BA patrol, some of whom reportedly talked of revenge for their '5 mates killed in South Armagh'. BA claim riot was taking place. Local witnesses say there was no disturbance until after the shooting.	21/5/81	BA	Deliberate Shooting	West Belfast
Henry Duffy	Shot by BA with plastic bullets in head & chest. D was walking home & not involved in rioting according to witnesses. He died 3 days after being shot.	25/5/81	BA	'Riot'	Derry City
Nora McCabe	Shot by BA with plastic bullet from range of 6 feet. Witnesses said she was on way to shops and not involved in rioting.	9/7/81	BA	'Riot'	West Belfast
Danny Barrett	Shot by BA sniper as he sat on wall outside his home in Ardoyne. (See Report, para.67)	9/7/81	BA	'Riot'	North Belfast
Peter Doherty	Shot by BA with plastic bullet as he stood in his kitchen. BA claimed he threw missiles from window but no one in house was questioned or charged.	31/7/81	BA	'Riot'	West Belfast

NAME	SUMMARY	DATE	AGENT	CATEGORY	PLACE
Peter Doherty (cont.)	Witnesses deny anything was thrown.	31/7/81	BA	'Riot'	West Belfast
Peter McGuinness	Shot by BA with plastic bullet during a riot. BA said he was a rioter, local witnesses say he tried to stop the riot.	9/8/81	BA	'Riot'	North Belfast
Martin Kyles	Shot by BA while joyriding in stolen car.	7/2/82	BA	Non-Political Criminal Activity	West Belfast
Stephen McConomy	11yr-old shot by BA with plastic bullet at range of 17 feet. (See Report, para. 76).	19/4/82	BA	'Accident'	Derry City
Eamonn Bradley	(See report, para. 60).	25/8/82	BA	Deliberate Shooting	Derry City
Ron Brennan	Shot by RUC in course of robbing post office. No shots were fired at RUC.	29/10/82	RUC	Deliberate Shooting.	Mallusk North Belfast
Gervaise McKerr Eugene Toman Sean Burns	(See report, para. 55).	11/11/82	RUC	Deliberate Shooting	Lurgan, Armagh
Michael Tighe	Shot by RUC at farm shed where he & Martin McCauley had found three 60yr-old rifles. RUC undercover patrol shot them without asking them to surrender. McC was wounded & charged with possession of firearm & conspiracy to murder.	24/11/82	RUC	Deliberate Shooting	County Armagh
Seamus Grew Roderick Carroll	(See Report, para. 54)	12/12/82	RUC	Deliberate Shooting	Armagh City
Patrick Elliott	(See Report, para. 68)	27/12/82	BA	Non-Political Criminal Activity	West Belfast
Francis McColgan	Shot by RUC during car chase following robbery of petrol station. RUC claim M & companions had imitation firearms.	19/1/83	RUC	Non-Political Criminal Activity	South Belfast
Eugene McMonagle	(See Report, para. 59)	3/2/83	BA	Deliberate Shooting	Derry City
William Millar	Shot by RUC undercover squad. Home-made sub-machine gun & pistol were found in car.	16/3/83	RUC	Non-Political Criminal Activity	South Belfast

NAME	SUMMARY	DATE	AGENT	CATEGORY	PLACE
Martin Malone	(See Report, para. 50)	30/7/83	UDR	Deliberate Shooting	Armagh City
Thomas Reilly	Shot by BA during questioning on street. Pvt. Ian Thaine was first serving soldier to be found guilty of murder for shooting a person while on duty in Northern Ireland. (December, 1984).	9/8/83	BA	Deliberate Shooting	West Belfast
Brigid Foster	(See Report, para. 52)	28/11/83	RUC	Deliberate Shooting.	Tyrone
Colm McGirr Brian Campbell	(See Report, para. 46)	4/12/83	BA	Stake-out at IRA arms dump.	Tyrone
Seamus Fitzsimmons	Shot by RUC during attempted robbery of Ballygally post office.	14/5/84	RUC	Attempted Robbery	Larne, Co.Antrim
John Downes	(See Report, para. 72)	12/8/84	RUC	Demonstration	West Belfast
Fred Jackson	Shot in crossfire between BA and IRA gunmen.	19/10/84	BA	Undercover Military Operation.	East Tyrone
Daniel Doherty William Fleming	IRA members shot by SAS while riding motor cycle in grounds of psychiatric hospital in Derry. BA said both men were on way to kill a part-time member of security forces.	6/12/84	BA	Undercover Military Operation	Derry City
Paul Gerard Kelly	Shot by UDR while joy-riding in stolen car which crashed into roadblock.	15/1/85	UDR	Non-Political Criminal Activity.	West Belfast
Gerard Logue	Shot by RUC while joy-riding in stolen car.	7/2/85	RUC	Non-Political Criminal Activity.	West Belfast

Appendix B

Individuals and Organisations who provided written testimony to the Inquiry.

1. Association for Legal Justice (Belfast):
   'Submission to the International Lawyers' Inquiry into the Lethal Use of Firearms by the Security Forces in Northern Ireland', 24 January 1984.

2. Kevin Boyle (Professor of Law, University College, Galway),

   Steven Greer (Cobden Trust Research Student, Faculty of Law, The Queen's University, Belfast),

   Tom Hadden (Lecturer in Law, The Queen's University, Belfast),

   Dermot Walsh (Lecturer in Law, University College, Cork):
   'Review of the Northern Ireland (Emergency Provisions) Act 1978', 1983.

3. Father Denis Faul, Father Raymond Murray:
   Plastic Bullets – Plastic Government: Deaths and Injuries by Plastic Bullets, August 1981 – October 1982, October 1982.
   Rubber and Plastic Bullets Kill and Maim: Violations of Human Rights by R.U.C. and British Army in Northern Ireland, August 1981.
   'Statement of Irish Bishops: Ban Plastic Bullets', July 1983.

4. Steven Greer (Cobden Trust Research Student, Faculty of Law, The Queen's University, Belfast),
   'Submission to the International Lawyers' Inquiry into the Use of Firearms by the Security Forces in Northern Ireland: The Law Governing the Use of Force by the Security Forces', January 1984.
   'A Report on the Inquest into the Death of Stephen McConomy', 30 June 1983.

5. Dr Tom Hadden (Lecturer in Law, The Queen's University, Belfast):
   'Coroners' Inquests on Disputed Killings in Northern Ireland: Memorandum prepared by the Committee on the Administration of Justice', 1983.

6. Haldane Society of Socialist Lawyers (Britain):
   'Justifiable Homicide: A Critical Comment on the Law Relating to the Use of Lethal Weapons by the Security Forces', January 1984.
   'Submissions to the Enquiry into the Workings of the Emergency Powers Legislation in Northern Ireland being conducted by Sir George Baker', 1983.
   'Emergency Powers: the Army and the Rule of Law', Nick Blake, Secretary of the Haldane Society, January 1984.

7. Paddy Hillyard (Lecturer in Social Administration, University of Bristol, England):
   'Evidence submitted to Sir George Baker's Review of the Northern Ireland (Emergency Provisions) Act 1978', August 1983.

8. Inquest: United Campaigns for Justice, London, England:
   'Coroners' Procedures in Northern Ireland: Evidence to the International Lawyers' Inquiry into the Lethal Use of Firearms by the Security Forces', January 1984.

9. Irish Information Partnership, Gondregnies, Belgium:
   'Submission of the Irish Information Partnership to the International Lawyers' Inquiry into the Lethal Use of Firearms by the Security Forces in Northern Ireland', January 1984.
   This Submission included the following Appendices:
   'Detailed Records of Civilian Casualties Caused by Members of the Security Forces in Northern Ireland: July 1969–July 1983.'
   'Disputed Casualties since 1971 (A Selection) Caused by Members of the Security Forces in Northern Ireland.'
   'Civilian Casualties Caused by Members of the Security Forces and Total Casualties Caused by Members of the Security Forces in Northern Ireland: Annual Totals from July 1969 to August 1983.'
   'Recent Trends in Violent Incidents and Casualties in Northern Ireland.'
   'Civilian Casualties by Various Agencies in Northern Ireland.'

10. National Council for Civil Liberties (Britain):
    'Submission to the International Lawyers' Inquiry into the Lethal Use of Firearms by the Security Forces in Northern Ireland', Terry Munyard, NCCL Executive Committee, February 1984.
    'Evidence prepared for a Review of the Northern Ireland (Emergency Provisions) Act 1978 to be conducted by the Rt Hon.

Sir George Baker OBE', September 1983.
'NCCL Briefing: The Prevention of Terrorism Bill 1983', Sarah Spencer, October 1983.

11. Northern Ireland Association of Socialist Lawyers:
'A Submission to the International Lawyers' Inquiry into the Lethal Use of Firearms by the Security Forces in Northern Ireland', February, 1984.

12. Northern Ireland Civil Rights Association:
'Case on the Denial of Civil Rights in Northern Ireland placed before the World Parliament of Peoples for Peace, Sofia, 1980', presented by Mrs Edwina Stewart, Honorary Secretary, NICRA.

Appendix C
Bibliography

General Histories

Beckett, J. C., *A Short History of Ireland*, 3rd ed., 1966.

Beckett, J. C., *The Making of Modern Ireland, 1603-1923*, Faber & Faber, London 1969.

Dangerfield, G., *The Damnable Question*, London 1979.

Farrell, M., *Northern Ireland: The Orange State*, 2nd ed., Pluto Press, London 1980.

Lyons, F. S. L., *Ireland Since The Famine: 1850 to the Present*, Fontana Books, London 1973.

McArdle, D., *The Irish Republic: A Documented Chronicle of the Anglo-Irish Conflict and the Partitioning of Ireland*, Gollancz, London 1937; Corgi, London 1968.

Moody, T. W. and Martin, F. X. (eds), *The Course of Irsh History*, Revised and enlarged edition, Mercier Press, Cork 1984.

Neeson, E., *The Civil War in Ireland, 1922-23*, Mercier Press, Cork 1966.

The Conflict from 1969 to the Present

Bell, J. Bowyer, *The Secret Army: A History of the IRA, 1916-1979*, Academy Press, Dublin 1979.

Bloch, J., & Fitzgerald, P., *British Intelligence and Covert Action: Africa, Middle East and Europe Since 1945*, Brandon, Dingle, Co. Kerry 1983.

Boulton, D., *The UVF 1966-73*, Gill & Macmillan, Dublin 1973.

Boyd, A., *Holy War in Belfast*, Anvil Books, Tralee, Co. Kerry 1969.

Boyd, A., *Northern Ireland: Who is to Blame?* Mercier Press, Cork 1984.

Clarke, A. F. N., *Contact*, Secker & Warburg, London 1983.

Coogan, T. P., *On the Blanket: The H-Block Story*, Ward River Press, Dublin, 1980.

Coogan, T. P., *The IRA*, Fontana Books, London, 1980.

Curtis, Liz, *Ireland: The Propaganda War*, Pluto Press, London 1984.

Curtis, Liz, *Nothing but the Same Old Story*, Information on Ireland Publication, London 1984.

Deutsch, R. & Magowan, V., *Northern Ireland: A Chronology of Events* (3 vol.) Blackstaff Press, Belfast 1974.

Devlin, B., *The Price of My Soul*, Pan Books, London 1969.

Dillon, M., & Lehane, D., *Political Murder in Northern Ireland*, Penguin Books, Harmondsworth, 1973.

Dunne, D., & Kerrigan, G., *Round Up the Usual Suspects*, Magill, Dublin 1984.

Fairweather, E., McDonough, R., & McFadyean, M., *Only the Rivers Run Free: Northern Ireland; the Women's War*, Pluto Press, London 1984.

Geraghty, T., *The Story of the Special Air Services 1950-1980*, Arms & Armour Press, London 1980.

Holland, J., *Too Long a Sacrifice*, Penguin Books, Harmondsworth 1981.

Kelley, K., *The Longest War: Northern Ireland and the IRA*, Zed Press, London 1982.

McArdle, P., *The Secret War*, Mercier Press, Cork 1984.

McCafferty, N., *The Armagh Women*, Co-op Books, Dublin, 1981.

McCann, E., *War and an Irish Town*, 2nd ed., Penguin Books, Harmondsworth, 1980.

McGuffin, J., *Internment*, Anvil Books, Tralee, Co. Kerry 1975.

O'Malley, P., *The Uncivil Wars*, Blackstaff Press, Belfast 1983.

Sunday Times Insight Team, *Ulster*, Penguin Books, Harmondsworth 1972.

Taylor, P., *Beating the Terrorists?*, Penguin Books, Harmondsworth 1980.

The Law and the Courts

Boyd, A., *The Informers*, Mercier Press, Cork 1984.

Boyle, K., Hadden, T., & Hillyard, P., *Law and State: The Case of Northern Ireland*, Martin Robertson, London 1975.

Boyle, K., Hadden, T., & Hillyard, P., *Ten Years On in Northern Ireland: the Legal Control of Political Violence*, Cobden Trust, London 1980.

Dash, S., *Justice Denied: A Challenge to Lord Widgery's Report on Bloody Sunday*, Defence and Education Fund of the International League for the Rights of Man in association with NCCL, London 1972.

Gifford, Lord T., *Inquiry into the circumstances surrounding the deaths of Seamus Cusack and George Desmond Beattie*, 1972.

Gifford, Lord T., *Death on the Streets of Derry*, NCCL, London 1983.

Gifford, Lord T., *Supergrasses: The use of accomplice evidence in Northern Ireland*, Cobden Trust, London 1984.

Harvey, R., *Diplock and the Assault on Civil Liberties*, Haldane Society, London 1981.

Pollack, A. (Ed.), *Fortnight Magazine: An Independent Review for Northern Ireland*: A reliable and increasingly regular source of information, especially on the courts, security forces and current events. Belfast, every two weeks, at present.

Scorer, S., & Hewitt, P., *The Prevention of Terrorism Act: The Case for Repeal*, NCCL, London 1981.

Spencer, S., *The Prevention of Terrorism Bill 1983*, NCCL, London 1983.

Walsh, D., *Arrest, Interrogation and Diplock Courts*, Cobden Trust, London 1983.

Workers' Research Unit, *Belfast Bulletin No. 10: The Law in Northern Ireland*, Belfast 1982.

Workers' Research Unit, *Belfast Bulletin No. 11: Supergrasses*, Belfast 1984.

British Government Reports

Disturbances in Northern Ireland: Report of the Commission appointed by the Governor of Northern Ireland (Cameron Report), HMSO Belfast, September 1969, Cmnd. 532.

Report of the Advisory Committee on Police in Northern Ireland (Hunt Report), HMSO Belfast, October 1969, Cmnd. 535.

Report of the Enquiry into Allegations against the Security Forces of Physical Brutality in Northern Ireland arising out of Events on 9th August 1971 (Compton Report), HMSO London, November 1971, Cmnd. 823.

Violence and Civil Disturbances in Northern Ireland in 1969: Report of Tribunal of Enquiry (Scarman Report), 2 Vols, HMSO Belfast, April 1972, Cmnd. 566.

Report of the Tribunal appointed to Enquire into the Events on Sunday 30th January 1972 which led to Loss of Life in connection with the Procession in Londonderry on that Day (Widgery Report), HMSO London, 1972 H.L.101/H.C.220.

Report of the Commission to consider Legal Procedures to deal with Terrorist Activities in Northern Ireland (Diplock Report), HMSO London, December 1972, Cmnd. 5185.

Report of a Committee to consider, in the Context of Civil Liberties and Human Rights, Measures to deal with Terrorism in North-ern Ireland (Gardiner Report), HMSO London, January 1975, Cmnd. 5847.

Review of the Operation of the Prevention of Terrorism (Temporary Provisions) Act 1976 (Shackleton Report), HMSO London, August 1978, Cmnd. 7342.

Report of the Committee of Inquiry into Police Interrogation Procedures in Northern Ireland (Bennett Report), HMSO London, March 1979, Cmnd. 7497.

Review of the Operation of the Prevention of Terrorism (Temporary Provisions) Act 1976 (Jellicoe Report), HMSO London, March 1983, Cmnd. 8803.

Review of the Operation of the Northern Ireland (Emergency Provisions) Act 1978 (Baker Report), HMSO London, April 1984, Cmnd. 9222.

Appendix D

International League of Human Rights Submission to the UN Sub-Commission on Prevention of Discrimination and Protection of Minorities

Thirty-Sixth Session

The Comments of the International League for Human Rights on the U.K. Government's response 29 August 1983 to International League's intervention under Agenda Item 9 concerning restraints in the use of force by law enforcement officials.

I. *Government of the UK:* 'These rounds are, moreover, used only when absolutely necessary'; 'I wish to make it clear that plastic bullet rounds have never been used in non-riot situations.'

International League: The most recent inquest opened on 17 June 1983 on the plastic bullet victims, that of Stephen McConomy, a boy of 11 years old, made the following findings:

(1) There was insufficient evidence to suggest that Stephen McConomy was rioting when he was shot;

(2) He was shot from a range of 17 feet when the minimum recommended range is 60 feet;

(3) The riot gun from which the plastic bullet was fired was faulty.

All 11 people killed have been Catholics. Inquests held in 1982 and 1983 have found that six of them were not involved in any disturbance which was going on at the time. The adjourned inquest into the death of Mrs Nora McCabe, the mother of two children, is almost certain to come to a similar finding. Thirty-years-old Mrs Nora McCabe was shot by the Royal Ulster Constabulary from just six feet way. In the cases of Stephen Geddis, aged 10 years, and Michael Donnelly, aged 20 years, the inquest made no findings on their involvement in disturbances, but on the evidence it seems unlikely that they were rioting.

The *Sunday Times* of London: Derek Humphry described the death of Stephen Geddis. He wrote: 'By all accounts Stephen was not one of the city's wild youngsters. He was withdrawn and rarely went outdoors, spending most of his time playing with toys and learning the guitar and mouth organ.' On 28 August 1975 a crowd of about 30 boys aged between 7 and 13 began stoning soldiers who were trying to remove some cushions the boys had set fire to in the road. Eye-witnesses said Stephen was not involved in the stoning. Then a soldier, pursuing a group of boys, fired a plastic bullet. Stephen, who was about 40 yards away, was hit on the head. He died 3 days later.

Carol Ann Kelly, aged 12, was hit on the side of the head by a plastic bullet fired by soldiers in a jeep on 19 May 1981. She was returning from a local shop with a carton of milk for her mother. Witnesses agreed that there was no rioting in the immediate area at the time. They said that when the soldiers came into the area they were very agitated. Five soldiers had been killed by a bomb that day in South Armagh and the soldiers were shouting at the residents, 'We'll get you for our five mates today.' At the the inquest on 21 May 1983 the coroner described Carol Ann Kelly as an 'innocent victim'.

Paul Whitters aged 15 years was involved in a disturbance on 15 April 1981; five civilian witnesses agreed that he was separated from stonethrowers at the time of the shooting, that he was hit by a plastic bullet fired by a policeman at close range, and they agreed that the police could easily have overpowered and arrested him.

On 28 August 1981 Paul Corr aged 12 years was shot by Royal Marine Commandos returning from a local shop to his home. There was no rioting in the area at the time. The plastic bullet caused severe physical injury requiring extensive plastic surgery.

II. *Government of the UK:* 'Their (The International League for Human Rights) reference to the use of these rounds indoors relates to an occasion on which a single member of the Security Forces was being seriously assaulted by a large crowd. The two plastic bullet rounds were fired at the ceiling in order to assist the recovery of the injured individual.'

International League: According to the *Irish News* a mainstream Belfast daily newspaper, on 12 October 1982 police entered the Lake Glen Hotel in West Belfast and fired plastic bullets at people who were there. Photographs published in the newspaper showed numerous plastic bullet marks on the interior walls of the hotel; many of these were at head level. Members of the public who were present and the hotel management described the police attack as unprovoked.

The firing of plastic bullets by the Royal Ulster Constabulary and the British Army inside social clubs has been reported on other occasions. For example, on 10 October 1976 British soldiers entered the Ballymurphy Working Men's Club, Belfast, in force. After some of the men present had objected to being photographed the soldiers opened fire with both live rounds and baton rounds. Five civilians were treated at the Royal Victoria Hospital, Belfast, for head wounds, one requiring 24 stitches.

At 9 am on 4 November 1971 a paratrooper, incensed by the playing of an Irish rebel record, fired a rubber bullet through the open window of the home of Mrs. Emma Groves, mother of 11 children. She was hit at about 8 yards range in the face. Both eyes had to be surgically removed.

On 24 July 1981 Peter Doherty was hit by a plastic bullet when he was in a first floor flat of a block of flats. He died on 31 July.

III. *Government of the UK:* 'The Security Forces in N. Ireland are entirely subject to the law and if a member is found to have used more force then was reasonable in particular circumstances he would be charged with a criminal offence. . . all incidents in which persons are killed or injured by Plastic Baton Rounds are fully investigated and a report is sent to the independent Director of Public Prosecutions who decides whether or not it would be appropriate to prefer charges. . . Any complaint against the police or army is also fully investigated and reports again must be submitted to the Director of Public Prosecutions; handling of these complaints is carefully monitored by the independent Police Complaints Board.'

International League: Under Northern Irish law there are remedies for the use of unreasonable force. Criminal complaints can be brought against the law enforcement official and the victim or his family can seek civil remedies for compensation. Substantial compensation has already been paid to rubber and plastic bullets victims in settlements 'out of court'. In most cases where a civil settlement has been reached, there has been no rigorous prosecution of the officers concerned and in no case has there been a conviction.

Although in individual cases there have been police-conducted investigations – albeit inadequate – we re-emphasise that a 'general public investigation' is needed. An overview is long overdue to assess generally the policy of using the plastic bullets as a riot control device. Since it was introduced into Northern Ireland in 1973, the plastic bullet has caused 11 deaths and numerous physical injuries. An independent and impartial inquiry could identify and evaluate possible existing patterns of abuse and recommend appropriate measures of reform.

IV. *UK Government:* 'I must take issue with their (International League for Human Rights) interpretation of United States Army Research. The U.S. findings were inconclusive and were in connection with a different type of projectile.'

International League: The plastic bullet at 50 yard range has an impact energy of 110 foot pounds. The United States army scientists categorised impact energies of more than 90 foot pounds as in the 'severe damage range'. A weapon with an almost identical impact energy as the plastic bullet, the 'stun-bag', was rejected by the scientists as 'unsatisfactory at all ranges'. Information regarding the impact energy of plastic bullets at ranges of 5, 15, 25, 50 yards were given in *Written Answers* by the British Secretary of State for Defence to British Parliamentary questions at a hearing on 21 January 1977. At 5 yards the plastic bullet has 285 foot pounds of energy and at 50 yards the energy of the projectile is still 149 foot pounds.

V. *UK Government:* 'Their (plastic bullets) use is also strictly monitored to ensure that these instructions are complied with.'

International League: There is no attempt to enforce controls particularly with regard to non-use at short ranges. Rounds must not be fired at a range of less than 20 metres and aiming at the lower part of the body. Yet deaths and serious injuries have been caused by firing at short range and at the head. Laurence Rocke of the Royal Victoria Hospital, Belfast, wrote in the medical journal *The Lancet* 23 April 1983 – 'My impression is that plastic bullets tend to cause more severe injuries to the skull and brain, and therefore more death.'

Appendix E

Northern Ireland Standing Advisory Commission on Human Rights

Excerpt from Annual Report for 1983 on the Use of Firearms by the Security Forces

1. The amount of force which may be used by any person, including the security forces is governed by section 3(1) of the Criminal Law Act (Northern Ireland) 1967 which provides:

> A person may use such force as is reasonable in the circumstances in the prevention of crime or in effecting or assisting in the lawful arrest of offenders or suspected offenders or persons unlawfully at large.

The law in England and Wales is stated in identical terms in section 3 of the Criminal Law Act, 1967. In addition, in both jurisdictions at common law, a person may use reasonable force in defence of himself and, in certain circumstances, in defence of another person.

2. Article 2 of the European Convention on Human Rights provides that everyone's right to life shall be protected by law but that 'deprivation of life shall not be regarded as inflicted in contravention of this Article when it results from the use of force which is no more than absolutely necessary:

> (a) in defence of any person from unlawful violence;
> (b) in order to effect a lawful arrest or to prevent escape of a person lawfully detained;
> (c) in action lawfully taken for the purpose of quelling a riot or insurrection.'

3. In its Report in 1965 the Criminal Law Revision Committee took the view that it was unnecessary to set out detailed rules on the use of force. They stated at paragraph 23:

> No doubt if a question arose on clause [now section] 3, the courts in considering what was reasonable force, would take into account all the circumstances, including in particular the nature and degree of force used, the seriousness of the evil to be prevented and the possibility of preventing it by other means; but there is no need to specify in the clause

the criteria for deciding the question. Since the clause is framed in general terms, it is not limited to arrestable or any other class of offences, though in the case of very trivial offences it would very likely be held that it would not be reasonable to use even the slightest force to prevent them.

However, during the last decade a number of cases involving the application of section 3 have arisen out of the civil disorder in Northern Ireland and it has been argued that the wording of this section is no longer adequate for the circumstances which have given rise to these incidents. In addition the Royal Commission on Criminal Procedure in England and Wales recognised generally in its 1981 Report that in order to perform their duty to investigate crime, the police needed to be provided with clear and specific powers to enable them to carry out such activities lawfully; the Royal Commission did not, however, review the operation of the law relating to the use of force in England and Wales nor recommend any amendment of section 3.

4. It has long been established in case law that where a suspect peacefully submits to the authority of a person making an arrest the use of force is not justified. But where the arrest is resisted either by confrontation or by flight, reasonable force may be used and would-be arresters are entitled to increase the amount of force employed in proportion to the resistance met and *may* ultimately be justified in killing the suspect. Similarly, in certain instances it may be legally permissible to kill a fleeing suspect. However, in order to justify use of force in such circumstances, there must exist an actual right of arrest, and the force used must always be reasonable in the circumstances.

5. The pivotal phrase in section 3(1) is therefore, 'such force as is reasonable in the circumstances.' This wording provides the legal test for determining whether the degree of force used on any particular occasion is justified. The 1967 Act provides no indication as to how this should be interpreted but Smith and Hogan in the leading *Text Book on Criminal Law* (5th edition 1983) suggest that it cannot be reasonable to cause death unless *(a)* it was necessary to do so in order to prevent the crime or effect the arrest *and (b)* the evil which would follow from failure to prevent the crime or effect the arrest is so great that a reasonable man might think himself justified in taking another's life to avert that evil.

6. The scope of section 3 may arise for consideration in both civil

and criminal cases – and may differ according to the context. It may therefore by possible for a shooting to be held unjustified (thus rendering a soldier liable in tort) while holding him not *criminally liable*. This distinction must be kept firmly in mind when considering the following cases in which the courts have commented on the meaning of this section.

7. *Farrell* v. *Secretary of State for Defence* [1979] A.C. 224 established that in section 3(1) it is the circumstances·directly affecting the person using the force which are to be considered; the words 'in the circumstances' relate solely to the immediate circumstances in which the force is used and it is not permissible to examine the preparatory steps which lead to force being used. In that case, following information received, four soldiers had been stationed at night on top of a building opposite a bank in anticipation of a bombing attack. Two men came to the bank and while placing money in the nightsafe three other men appeared and attempted to rob them. The soldiers, thinking that this was a bombing raid called on the robbers to halt. They did not and were shot dead. The plaintiff, the widow of one of those killed, sued the Ministry of Defence for damages, alleging trespass and negligence by the soldiers. The jury, in the High Court, found *inter alia* that it was reasonable in the circumstances to shoot to kill in the prevention of crime and in effecting the lawful arrest of the three men. The plaintiff appealed to the Northern Ireland Court of Appeal, which ordered a new trial on all issues on the ground *inter alia* that consideration should be given to 'the circumstances in which the operation was conceived and planned as well as those in which the decisive act was performed.' The Ministry of Defence then appealed to the House of Lords which in turn rejected the Court of Appeal's construction of section 3(1). Viscount Dilhorne stated:

> [section 3(1)] . . . can only provide a defence for those who used force and if the force the four soldiers used was reasonable in the circumstances in which they used it, the defects, if there were any, in the planning of the operation would not deprive them of that defence and render the force used unreasonable.

As a result the High Court's decision, rejecting the plaintiff's claim, was restored.

8. The plaintiff complained to the European Commission of Human Rights, submitting that the test of legality of the use of lethal

force in the domestic proceedings, namely whether it was in the circumstances reasonable to kill, involved a standard lower than that of absolute necessity enshrined in Article 2 (right to life) of the European Convention on Human Rights. She also complained of a breach of Articles 6 (right to a fair hearing) and 13 (effective remedy before a national authority) of the Convention. The Commission in December 1982 declared that the application under Article 2 was admissible but that the claims under Article 6 and Article 13 were inadmissible. The Commission is now considering the merits of the case with a view to securing a friendly settlement.* If such a solution is not reached, the Commission will draw up a report and state its opinion as to whether the facts disclose a breach by the United Kingdom of its obligations under the Convention. This report will be transmitted to the Committee of Ministers which will decide the matter, unless the case is referred to the European Court of Human Rights by the Commission or the United Kingdom.

9. In *R. v. MacNaughton* (1975) an army sergeant was in charge of a patrol in a hostile border area. An explosion was heard and shortly afterwards a man was met coming from the direction of the blast. He was arrested on suspicion of being implicated. According to the prosecution the man was then ordered to go to one side and was summarily shot by the defendant. This was denied by the defendant, who said that the man had tried to escape and he had only shot him after calling on him to halt. The Lord Chief Justice (Lord Lowry) held that the defendant's story might reasonably be true and stated that, to avail himself of the defence that the force used was reasonable in the circumstances, a defendant must raise a 'triable issue'. The Lord Chief Justice did not explain what evidence is required to raise a 'triable issue', and there is some uncertainty in the case law on this point. It would seem, however, that a defendant charged with using excessive force must:

(a) put forward facts which contain the constituent elements of the defence; and
(b) adduce evidence sufficient to put before a jury.

Whether the defendant succeeds in doing so is a question for the judge to decide. It is for the jury (if there is one in the case) to consider as a question of fact whether the force used in the circumstances was reasonable. The test of what is 'reasonable' is an objective one

* Mrs Farrell has now received an out-of-court 'friendly settlement' of £27,000. The report which forms the basis of the settlement is not publicly available.

and the circumstances to be considered are those which the defendant reasonably and honestly believed to exist at the time of his actions.

10. In the *Attorney-General for Northern Ireland's Reference* (1976) Jones L.J. approved the following summary of the law:

> . . . the question of reasonable force is to be decided objectively, but having regard to the circumstances in which the person concerned. . . was and the conditions which *he* reasonably thought existed [This]. . . contains objective and subjective elements.

According to Lord Diplock, in the same case, the question 'what amount of force is reasonable in the circumstances?' is always for the jury and never a point of law for the judge. Lord Diplock stated the question for the jury as follows:

> Are we satisfied that no reasonable man *(a)* with knowledge of such facts as were known to the accused or reasonably believed by him to exist *(b)* in the circumstances and time available to him for reflection *(c)* could be of the opinion that the prevention of the risk of harm to which others might be exposed if the suspect were allowed to escape, justified exposing the suspect to the risk of harm to him that might result from the kind of force that the accused contemplated using.

In that case the defendant was a member of a patrol searching for terrorists in an area where there had been a great deal of paramilitary activity, and where there was always the threat of an ambush. During the search the defendant came across a man who was unarmed but whom the defendant suspected was a terrorist. The defendant called the man to stop but he ran away and the defendant shot him dead. The defendant was acquitted of murder after testifying that he believed the man was in the Provisional I.R.A. and there was a danger that he might pass on the whereabouts of the patrol to his confederates who might then mount an ambush. The Crown contended that the shooting could not be justified in the absence of a belief that the dead man had either been involved in acts of terrorism or that he was likely to be involved in such acts in the immediate future. But this limitation was rejected by the Court of Appeal and the House of Lords. Lord Diplock said that on the facts there was material upon which a tribunal of fact might take the view that the defendant had reasonable grounds for apprehension of imminent danger to himself and other members of the patrol if the deceased were allowed to escape.

11. The standard of reasonableness to be applied, according to

Smith and Hogan, should not be a strict one. As Holmes J. said in the case of *Brown* v. *USA* (1921), 'detached reflection cannot be demanded in the presence of an uplifted knife', and Lord Diplock, in *Attorney-General for Northern Ireland's Reference* (1976) said:

> ... The postulated balancing of risk against risk, harm against harm, by the reasonable man is not undertaken in the calm analytical atmosphere of the court-room after counsel with the benefit of hindsight have expounded at length the reasons for and against the kind and degree of force that was used by the accused; but in the brief second or two which the accused had to decide whether to shoot or not and under all the stresses to which he was exposed.

In balancing out the risks, the defendant was not only entitled to take into account a short-term or imminent threat, but

> ... the killing or wounding by members of the patrol by terrorists in ambush, and the effects of his success by members of the Provisional I.R.A. in encouraging the continuance of the armed insurrection and all the misery and destruction of life and property that terrorist activity in Northern Ireland had entailed.

12. That the defendant's belief in the nature of the circumstances must be reasonable as well as honest is also illustrated by the case of *McGuigan* v. *Ministry of Defence* (1982). In this civil case, the plaintiff had been shot in the chest by two soldiers in an observation post. There had been frequent attacks on the security forces in the area including two explosions in the vicinity of the post on the evening in question. The plaintiff was shot as he emerged from an alleyway. The defendants alleged that he was armed at the time and claimed that the shooting was justified on the grounds of self defence and under section 3(1) as amounting to no more than reasonable force in the circumstances. Allowing the plaintiff's claim, the trial judge held that on the evidence it was clear that the plaintiff had not been armed. Where self defence and section 3(1) were relied on as a defence to a civil claim the onus of proof was on the defence to show on the balance of probabilities that the assault was justified and that the force used was reasonable. It was not enough that the defendants honestly believed that the plaintiff was armed; they had to show reasonable grounds for that belief. Accordingly they had failed to provide justification, and the plaintiff was entitled to damages, assessed at £15,000 for pain and suffering and £13,122 for loss of earnings.

13. As to the seriousness of the crime to be prevented by the use of force, recent cases in Northern Ireland show that the means used to effect an arrest should not be disproportionate to the evil to be prevented. Thus a policeman shooting a shoplifter to prevent his escape or shooting while in pursuit of someone believed to have committed an indecent assault would normally constitute clear examples of disproportionate force. Other cases, such as the use of lethal force to prevent robbery, are more problematic. The difficulty stems from the fact that section 3(1) does not explicitly contain an element of proportionality.

14. In accordance with the decisions of the House of Lords in *Attorney-General for Northern Ireland's Reference* and in *Farrell* v. *Secretary of State for Defence,* the existence of an alternative and potentially less violent means of preventing an evil or carrying out an arrest may be relevant.

15. In *R.* v. *Bohan and Temperley* soldiers keeping watch on an arms cache shot a boy (John Boyle) who was examining one of the weapons, in the reasonable but mistaken belief that it was aimed at them. The Lord Chief Justice criticised the execution of the operation and said that an alternative approach might have obviated the need for the killing, but it was recognised that operations by the security forces in Northern Ireland are often conducted in potentially hostile areas with a greater risk to safety. However, the judgment finding the defendants not guilty was based on the issue of self defence, as distinct from the alternative defence based on section 3 that the defendants had used reasonable force in the prevention of crime. But like section 3, the defence of self defence involves both subjective and objective elements. Thus, Halsbury says:

> There must be a reasonable necessity for the killing, or at least an honest belief based on reasonable grounds that there was a necessity.

In the light of this case the issue of self defence would seem to require only two questions to be resolved. The first question is one of fact – what did the defendant honestly and reasonably believe? The second is one of law – does the defendant's belief, if true, justify his action? The essence of self defence is that the defendant inflicts harm on his victim to save himself from harm – but should the same consideration apply to a policeman or soldier faced by a man waving a gun, as apply to an ordinary person faced with a physical attack? It has, for instance, been suggested that self defence should never be considered in any attempt to justify the use of firearms or of any lesser degree of force by the police. This seems to be going too far – but there is an obvious need for consistency in the application of section 3 and the scope of the defence of self defence.

16. The circumstances surrounding security operations were a critical consideration for the judge in another civil case – *Lynch* v. *Ministry of Defence*. The plaintiff in that case had been struck by a number of bullets fired by two soldiers after he refused to stop the stolen car he was driving when an army patrol requested him to do so. The Ministry of Defence contended that the force used by the soldiers was reasonable in the circumstances in the defence of other soldiers, and by virtue of section 3 of the Criminal Law Act (Northern Ireland) 1967, the force used by the soldiers was also reasonable in the circumstances in effecting or attempting to effect the lawful arrest of the plaintiff as an offender or suspected offender. The trial judge held that it had not been shown, on the balance of probabilities, that the car the plaintiff was driving deliberately attempted to run down and kill or seriously injure any of the soldiers or that the soldiers who fired had reasonable grounds for believing that that was what the car was doing. Therefore the defence that they had fired to protect the lives of the other soldiers failed. Further, the court was not satisfied that the soldiers reasonably suspected the driver of having committed an offence which would justify opening fire to effect his arrest for that offence and therefore the court was equally not satisfied that the firing constituted reasonable force in effecting the lawful arrest of a suspected offender. The plaintiff's claim was dismissed however because it was clear that the plaintiff deliberately decided to disobey a signal from a soldier to stop and therefore on the balance of probabilities it was shown that when the soldiers fired they believed, and had reasonable grounds for believing, that the driver of the car was a terrorist who was anxious to avoid being stopped by the patrol. Moreover, having regard to the very frequent use of motor vehicles by terrorist organisations for the purpose of committing the gravest crimes in Northern Ireland, the firing of shots by the soldiers amounted to the use of reasonable force in the circumstances in the prevention of crime.

17. In holding that the force used was reasonable in the circumstances of *R.* v. *MacNaughton* the Lord Chief Justice said:

> It is vitally important to remember that the patrol was working in active service conditions and I do not refer to the mere mounting of road

blocks or the undertaking of routine patrols. Judging by the events of 1972 and 1973 in this area, the section was operating in hostile country, and judging further by the explosion, it was operating in the possible presence of an ambush. These facts make a great difference, to my mind in assessing whether shooting at an escaping prisoner was a reasonable way of dealing with the situation.

18. In a civil case involving the use of force, in addition to, or as an alternative to the question of whether it was reasonable in the circumstances under section 3, the issue of whether such force was used negligently may constitute a separate head of claim. In W. v. *Ministry of Defence* a schoolgirl while sitting in a neighbour's kitchen had been struck in the face by a plastic baton round fired by a soldier. There had been some rioting in the area at the time, but the judge held that the baton round had been fired in a negligent fashion in that it had not been aimed at a carefully designated target in such a manner as to strike the lower part of the body and it had not been fired at a target which was within accurate firing range.

19. Both the Royal Ulster Constabulary and the Armed Services have issued instructions to members governing the use of firearms. If a member of the security forces contravenes these rules he commits a disciplinary, but not necessarily a criminal, offence or a civil wrong. The precise details of these instructions are not public knowledge.

20. Comparisons have recently been drawn between incidents in the Province and a shooting in London involving the Metropolitan police. The London shooting had led to the immediate suspension from duty of three police officers, a statement to parliament by the Home Secretary, the speedy preparation and submission of a preliminary report to the Director of Public Prosecutions and criminal charges being brought against police officers.

21. The very different threat posed to the security forces in Northern Ireland precludes direct comparisons with events in England. The dangers faced by members of the security forces were indeed brought sharply into focus [at the time the Commission considered this subject] when two police officers were shot dead and a third injured outside a post office in Rostrevor as they approached a suspicious car. Nevertheless uncertainty about the rights and duties of the security forces in Northern Ireland may stem from the fact that not only are the security forces' instructions not public knowledge but that the ordinary law has to be applied in circumstances with which it was not designed to cope. It must therefore be

considered whether section 3 of the Criminal Law Act (Northern Ireland) 1967 should be amended so as to define more precisely and comprehensively the circumstances in which it would be reasonable for the security forces to use potentially lethal force.

Standing Advisory Commission on Human Rights,
31 October 1983.

Note of Acknowledgment

The work of the Inquiry was facilitated in many ways by people too numerous to mention by name, especially those witnesses who gave valuable evidence, oral and written, in Northern Ireland. The Report could not have been produced without generous financial support from many sources and the final publication owes a great deal to the enthusiasm, efficiency and unfailing courtesy of Mary Feehan of The Mercier Press.

The stature of the Inquiry also benefited from the wide and representative endorsement which it received from a number of human rights and civil liberties organisations in Ireland, Britain and the United States.

The members of the Inquiry would be remiss in the extreme if they did not specifically refer to the concrete and substantial contributions of a number of individuals. In New York, Paul O'Dwyer and Frank Durcan provided invaluable support and Mary Rehill worked tirelessly in the typing of various drafts. In Northern Ireland, the officers and members of the Association for Legal Justice assisted in the making of arrangements and their knowledge of, familiarity with and contacts in all parts of the North were invaluable. Steven Greer, Cobden Trust Research Student, Faculty of Law, The Queen's University of Belfast, apart from submitting two excellent papers to the Inquiry, responded to our requests for assistance promptly and very efficiently. In Dublin, Louise Asmal offered encouragement and assistance, while Gerard Hogan, Lecturer in Law, Trinity College Dublin, Eanna Molloy and Olive Murtagh helped with the final draft in various ways.

In an even more comprehensive sense, the Inquiry is indebted to Richard Harvey and Marlene Archer, secretaries and counsel to the Inquiry. In countless respects, the Report bears the imprint of their influence and dedication. They struggled hard to meet a great array of requests made by the Inquiry, mostly large and some small and assured arrangements, facilities, documentation and information that enabled us to carry out the job of investigating in a manner at once efficient and pleasant.

Despite the anguish of dealing with the terrible human and

personal ordeal caused by the events in Northern Ireland and the delicate nature of its undertaking, the Inquiry was sustained by the generosity of spirit of all those, lawyers and non-lawyers, especially in Northern Ireland, who gave written and oral evidence and assisted the Inquiry.

The Informers

A Chilling Account of the Supergrasses
in Northern Ireland

Andrew Boyd

' . . . the latest in a long line of discredited legal strategies, which included internment and the Castlereagh interrogation centres.'
Association of Socialist Lawyers

' . . . a travesty of both legal and natural justice.'
Martin Flannery, MP

' . . . the courts themselves are on trial.'
The Times, 13 September 1983

' . . . uncorroborated evidence, unsafe evidence, and dangerous evidence was being relied upon.'
Gene Turner from the US Congress

'The practice of giving immunity to the most terrible terrorists and then using their uncorroborated evidence to put someone else in prison is bound to bring the law, those who make the law, and those who enforce the law into total disrepute.'
·Councillor Sam Wilson, DUP

'Most of the checks for people to prove their innocence have been done away with. I'm very concerned with the situation.'
Noël Saint-Pierre of the Québec Jurists Association

With one hand extended in what appears to be gestures of reform and conciliation and the other encased in the mailed gauntlet of repression the British have blundered through another fifteen years of political violence. Now they have turned to the use of informers.

The Irish Criminal Process

Edward F. Ryan and Philip Magee

This major work by two practising barristers represents the first attempt in over thirty years to provide both legal practitioners and students with a comprehensive picture of the Irish criminal process as it relates to serious offences. The years since 1950 have witnessed unprecedented developments in this area of law. Not only have there been extensive statutory changes in relation to search and seizure, extradiction, committal proceedings, free legal aid, the jury and the Special Criminal Courts but also the increasing invocation of the Constitution in the Criminal Courts has resulted in a welter of case law in the areas of arrest, bail, habeas corpus, the exclusion of certain evidence and rights of appeal.

Written in a clear, expository style, *The Irish Criminal Process* includes chapters on the structure and jurisdiction of the Irish courts, the right to prosecute, arrest, the gathering of evidence by the prosecution (i.e. questioning, confessions, identification procedures, search and seizure etc.), bail, legal representation, the preliminary hearing, the indictment, arraignment, the jury, the structure of the trial and various important evidentiary matters which may arise during it, sentence and appeals. The authors have also included chapters on State Side Orders and the Special Criminal Court. An attempt has been made to cite nearly every Irish case which remains of relevance and, especially in those areas where there exists a paucity of Irish material, the authors have made frequent reference to a host of authorities and illustrative material drawn from other jurisdictions, especially from the United Kingdom and the United State of America.

Whilst all concerned with the administration of the criminal law should find it useful the work is designed primarily for students and practitioners and the latter in particular will be interested in the inclusion of a comprehensive Table of Indictable Offences which will afford them quick reference to the maximum penalties which the courts may impose. The book contains an extensive index as well as lists of cases and statutes and numerous useful appendices.

Company Law in Ireland
Michael Forde

This major work on the law relating to companies is the first comprehensive treatise to be published in Ireland on this subject. It is written to satisfy the needs of barristers and solicitors who work in the companies field, accountants, company secretaries, other persons who are involved in the management of companies, and students of the subject.

In the past English books on company law sufficed to explain the legal position in this country. But the law on this topic in Britain and in Ireland has diverged over the last twenty years to such an extent that practitioners, business persons and students need a book on the Irish Companies Acts, 1963-1983. Dr Forde's *Company Law in Ireland* meets this need. As well as providing a complete analysis of the law in Ireland up to the end of 1984, incorporating the important Companies (Amendement) Act, 1983, this book incorporates particularly significant developments in the United States, Canada, Australia and New Zealand.

Dr Forde is a Barrister at Law and lectures on Company Law at University College, Dublin. During his academic career he studied at Trinity College, Dublin; Clare College, Cambridge; the Free University of Brussels; Yale Law School; and the King's Inns. He has taught law in the University of Chicago Law School, the University of Durham, and at University College, Cork. He has published extensively on various legal topics in some of the world's principal academic law journals.

www.ingramcontent.com/pod-product-compliance
Lightning Source LLC
Chambersburg PA
CBHW021145090426
42740CB00008B/944